Menaboni's Birds

Menaboni's

BY ATHOS AND SARA

FOREWORD BY JOHN FARRAND, JR.

EDITOR OF *AMERICAN BIRDS*
NATIONAL AUDUBON SOCIETY

Birds

MENABONI

PORTLAND HOUSE

NEW YORK

Dedicated to our mothers and fathers

This 1988 edition is published by Portland House, a
division of dilithium Press, Ltd. distributed by
Crown Publishers, Inc., 225 Park Avenue South,
New York, New York 10003, by arrangement with
Clarkson N. Potter, Inc.

Manufactured in Japan

Library of Congress Cataloging-in-Publication Data

Menaboni, Athos, 1895–
  [Birds]
  Menaboni's birds / by Athos and Sara Menaboni ;
foreword by John Farrand, Jr.
  ISBN 0-517-66295-7
  1. Birds—United States. 2. Menaboni, Athos,
1895- . 3. Animal painters—United States—
Biography. I. Menaboni, Sara. II. Title.
III. Title: Birds.
[QL682.M46 1988]
598.2973—dc19   87-37607
                                                      CIP

h g f e d c b a

LIST OF COLOR PLATES

Complete descriptive captions for the color
illustrations will be found on pages 149–156.

Grateful acknowledgment is made to the following owners of original Menaboni paintings
for permission to reproduce their paintings in this book:

Mr. Robert W. Woodruff (*eastern bluebird, mallard, killdeer, bobwhite,
mourning dove, northern oriole, belted kingfisher, and bufflehead*)

Mrs. Charles E. Thwaite, Jr. (*American robin*)

Judge and Mrs. John S. Langford, Jr. (*barn swallow*)

Mr. and Mrs. F. M. Bird, Jr. (*bobolink*)

Mrs. Hugh M. Scott (*hooded warbler*)

Dr. and Mrs. E. Garland Herndon, Jr. (*northern flicker*)

Mr. and Mrs. Joseph W. Jones (*hooded merganser*)

General and Mrs. James Grizzard (*bald eagle and snowy egret*)

Mr. and Mrs. Everett Bean (*wood duck*)

Mr. and Mrs. Forrest L. Adair III (*painted bunting*)

Miss Tina Menaboni (*least tern*)

Mr. and Mrs. John R. Ridley (*green-winged teal*)

The Atlanta Historical Society, Margaret Demmon Sims Collection
(*pileated woodpecker, Carolina chickadee, American kestrel, boat-tailed grackle,
red-winged blackbird, purple gallinule, and brown thrasher*)

Mr. and Mrs. Athos Menaboni (*wild turkey, common raven, Canada goose,
blue jay, and cardinal*)

Special thanks to the late Joe Reiner, who made this new edition possible

Hooded Merganser

John Burroughs was sitting on the porch of his next-door neighbor when she complained: "Why is it that you, Mr. Burroughs, have so many birds at your place but I do not have any in my yard?"

He had been watching the birds in her trees and shrubs, and he replied: "You will not see birds in your yard until you have birds in your heart."

Blue Jay

FOREWORD

$\mathcal{A}$THOS MENABONI holds a unique position among America's many painters of birds. He was born and raised in Livorno, Italy, and received his early artistic training from two great muralists, the Italian Ugo Manaresi and Charles Doudelet of Belgium. When he arrived in the United States as a young man, he brought with him the fruits of this European background. He admires the work of many bird painters of the United States and Canada, but as the splendid paintings in this volume show, he cannot be placed in any school or tradition of American bird art. His style is purely his own—bold, colorful, and joyful. For such freshness and originality, one must go back to the work of John James Audubon.

As his wife, Sara, relates in the chapters that accompany these bird portraits, Athos took up the painting of birds long after he had developed the keen and discerning eye of an artist. Although birds had been incorporated into many of his murals, he had never painted a bird portrait until one day, almost casually, he decided to paint a pair of cardinals—a species he had observed many times since his arrival in the United States. He painted the portrait without a cardinal in front of him, drawing on his vivid recollection of an intimate acquaintance with this familiar southern bird. The painting was intended to hang on the wall in the Menabonis' apartment, but was quickly purchased by an interior decorator. However, Athos had found such joy in creating that first painting, and in studying the birds themselves, that he embarked on a career that has left a profound mark on this specialized branch of art.

Before long his work was being exhibited at the American Museum of Natural History and at the National Audubon Society in New York, as well as in many galleries around the country. A large audience came to know his paintings, but for several years they hung only in galleries and in private collections. A still larger audience had yet to see them.

Then, in 1950, a little more than a decade after that first painting of the two cardinals, Rinehart and Company published *Menaboni's Birds*, a collection of 45 of his portraits in color and black and white, as well as numerous decorative drawings including birds and a delightful assortment of other natural objects—a luna moth, mushrooms, flowers, and delicately drawn leaves. In his introduction, "J.S.,"—John Selby, then editor-in-chief at Rinehart—told the story of Athos Menaboni's background and of how the book had come into being. Sara Menaboni contributed a warm and sensitive narrative of the Menabonis' encounters with birds and other wild creatures, both at home and on trips to distant parts of the United States and to other countries.

For me, as for many another youngster just beginning to learn his birds during those years, the appearance of that first edition of *Menaboni's Birds* had a very special meaning. To identify the birds around my childhood home in Connecticut, I had an excellent field guide, whose plates and text I knew by heart. But the paintings in it were carefully designed for field identification and not to show the birds in vibrant action, the way I saw them on my daily walks through the woods and fields. When I found *Menaboni's Birds* under the Christmas tree, I felt as though I had also found a kindred spirit. Here were the birds, painted as I knew them, painted as creatures of color and life. Here were two blue jays, dashing and inquisitive, scolding a snake among the branches of an oak tree. Here was a pair of red-winged blackbirds, the male displaying his fiery red epaulets just as I had seen these birds doing in a cattail marsh near my house. Here, too, were birds I had not yet seen; but from Menaboni's portrait of two pileated woodpeckers I knew what to expect—a large and dramatic bird, quick and alert in its movements, and clad in black and white with a flaming red crest.

What sets the paintings of Athos Menaboni apart from the work of other bird artists is, I think, the ability of the artist to convey not only the bird, but his own delight in the subject. Each painting is a very personal celebration of the joy he has found in birds—a joy that is familiar to all those who love them. Years later, I encountered a line of Henry David Thoreau's and thought at once of Menaboni. "A man's interest in a single bluebird," Thoreau wrote, "is worth more than a complete but dry list of the fauna and flora of a town."

For Athos and Sara Menaboni, the town was Atlanta, Georgia. In the early years of World War II, the Menabonis had moved into a quiet country retreat just a few miles from the city limits. They called their place Valle Ombrosa, the "Shady Valley," partly inspired by Vall'Ombrosa, the name of a beautiful town in the hills above Florence. Here Athos found the peace he needed to work on his bird portraits, and here Sara set out to record her own intense responses to the natural world.

In one of the chapters in the book Sara writes that it was her husband who opened her eyes to the manifold beauty of nature, and she even confesses: "With so much happening constantly and unexpectedly how can I put my thoughts in a neat and orderly pattern?" But this is an obstacle that every nature writer must surmount, and her style is as fresh and evocative as her husband's paintings. Seldom has a husband and wife team produced a book so well integrated and of such enduring value.

During the years since 1950, Athos Menaboni's paintings have been shown in galleries across the country, from the Lester K. Henderson Gallery in Monterey, California, to the Vose Gallery in Boston. But they have not appeared in book form since that first edition of *Menaboni's Birds*, published more than three decades ago. A whole generation has grown up without ready access to the work of this prolific and sensitive artist. The publication of this new edition is therefore a very special event. Through this book, Athos Menaboni will gain many new admirers, while for those of us who remember the first edition, it is like finding a long-time friend, still absorbed in the joy of his life's work.

In this new edition, Sara Menaboni's original text and John Selby's introduction are reprinted, along with the black and white drawings, but all of the color plates are new. And one, the portrait of the cardinals, is very new indeed. It was Athos's gift to Sara for Christmas, 1983. It is fitting that this should be the newest Menaboni painting, for it was the cardinal, so many years ago, that inspired Athos Menaboni to embark upon his career as a painter of birds.

Athos and Sara Menaboni still live at Valle Ombrosa, close to nature and close to the birds they both love so deeply. In Chapter 11 of this book, Sara writes of the coming of spring to Valle Ombrosa many years ago. It is spring as I write these lines. Once again, the brown thrashers are singing at Valle Ombrosa, and the columbines are coming up. Athos Menaboni is still hard at work, still giving us cause to reflect upon those long-ago lines of Fra Lippo Lippi:

We're made so, that we love
First, when we see them painted, things we have passed
Perhaps a hundred times, nor cared to see.

It is a special pleasure to write the foreword for this new edition of *Menaboni's Birds* and to wish Athos and Sara Menaboni many more springs at Valle Ombrosa.

New York   John Farrand, Jr.

Menaboni's Birds

Bobolink

INTRODUCTION FROM THE ORIGINAL EDITION

*T*HE REMARKABLE refusal of the interested public to lie quiet with the truth has begun a legend in Athos Menaboni's case. The legend is that Menaboni, whose paintings of birds have achieved the widest circulation in the last ten years, really began painting birds in the late 'thirties. That is, of course, nonsense.

One does not acquire the gift of accurately representing birds in colors and draftsmanship that make it seem the birds just have alighted for a look at their public. Menaboni has been observing birds (and for that matter animals) almost since his birth fifty-odd years ago in Livorno. The brightness and freshness of the hundreds of bird paintings that have rushed from his brush in recent years are the result of long experimentation, and for that matter, of a great experience in all departments of his art—from the days when he decorated candles for twelve important dollars a week in a New York loft to the present, when he might not satisfy all those who want a Menaboni painting if he worked with twelve hands instead of the conventional two.

Also they are the result of a peculiar and inward way of life. Athos Menaboni is no recluse; just the same, I suspect he could be quite content with his work, his wife Sara, and himself. It is impossible to find him in art galleries, even those that hang his paintings. I never have seen him trailing old ladies to pick up their gushing comment, and he is notoriously bad at buttering up possible clients. He simply will not go to cities, excepting occasionally to Atlanta, near which city he lives in a wooded sanctuary the Menabonis call Valle Ombrosa. The outside world goes to Valle Ombrosa in streams, and is welcome—but on the Menaboni terms. The terms are simple: one must respect and not interfere with Athos's work, and one must understand the feeling the Menabonis have for birds, for all the small creatures. This feeling is, quite simply, love.

When Athos was born in Livorno in 1895 his father, Averado Menaboni, (who always was called Babbò) was a ship chandler and the prosperous business he conducted was more than sufficient to provide a good way of life. Athos was the second of five children, four of whom still live. Babbo was a great hunter, and when Athos was not squatting in the walled garden watching a hill of ants or perhaps the family's pet falcon hunting mice, he was quite likely to be trotting around the hills acting as a two-legged retriever for his father.

Eventually the boy was given a specially made gun of his own, and still later a full-sized weapon. He shoots astonishingly well to this day, although he employs his skill in new ways, nowadays. Babbo was not only a hunter—he loved birds and animals, and constantly used Athos as an excuse to bring them home. Athos remembers a mongoose, a marten, a monkey, a Siberian wolf, dozens of dogs and at one time more than fifty birds.

These last attracted the boy too strongly. He spent nearly all his time with them instead of with his studies, and he was eventually punished by Jenny Menaboni, his mother, who ordered the lot released. Athos was broken hearted, until one of the birds returned. It was a sparrow, and when Babbo had quietly slipped his son enough money to refill the cages, and when once more the cages were emptied, this same sparrow returned to Athos and stayed staunchly by him. It is a little odd that one of the most affecting stories Sara Menaboni tells in this book is about still another sparrow—the Charlotte who lived out her days in the Menabonis' house.

It was evident to the family that Athos had

a talent for art, but before he was allowed to study, he spent one long summer in the original Vall'Ombrosa working out his lessons alone and spending every possible minute out of doors with birds. It did as much, that summer, as anything else in Menaboni's life to set him on his true path.

The boy was put to study with Ugo Manaresi, and with the Belgian Charles Daudelet. Daudelet accepted him characteristically.

"No," he said, "I will not take Athos as a pupil. If he has talent I shall take him as an apprentice."

So the boy was set to drawing a statue, and after an hour Daudelet returned, took the drawing away from him, and put his new apprentice to work filling in the green on a huge mural of the Holy Land then being repainted in his equally huge studio. Athos's work at the Royal Academy of Art in Florence was more or less conventional, but what he did with the things he learned was always the concern of one person only. Meaning Athos himself.

The first World War came, and for four years the young painter fought in the Italian army, acquiring a decoration and a fierce detestation for the process of organized killing that has grown even more intense with the years. After the war, he returned to Livorno and his family, and there he stayed for a couple of years until in the course of business an American freighter captain named John Hashagen was brought to the house, and eventually offered Athos the chance to sail with him. It seemed a good thing to a young man in his mid-twenties, even though Hashagen was not allowed to accept paying passengers, and had to sign on his young friend as a wiper.

There were two weeks in North Africa, and then the ship was ordered to Norfolk, and tied up for good. The first officer offered to be responsible for Athos, and since there were no immigration quotas then Athos went to New York and began painting candles at twelve dollars weekly

rather than write home for money. Four years later he was supporting himself very neatly as a painter of murals—he still likes to paint murals, by the way, and some of his most original work is in that field. Athos was not satisfied, just the same. Perhaps it was something in the blood from the days when the Menaboni family split in Florence over the Guelf and Ghibelline feud and one section emigrated to Livorno. Or something from the maternal grandfather who was a captain with Garibaldi.

In any case, the Florida boom was on, and when Athos was offered a position as art director of Davis Island, in Tampa Bay, he took it. He was also, for a while, an architectural sculptor in Fort Myers, and then (and swiftly) he was just a young man out of a job, because the boom flattened out under him and some hundreds of thousands more. He was offered a minor painting commission in Atlanta, and he took it for the best reason in the world. He was hungry.

In Atlanta he made some good friends: Philip Shutze the achitect, J. J. Haverty the art patron, and Mrs. Charles Jerome, then director of the High Museum of Art. These friends took over the job of finding commissions for the newcomer so that he could remain in Atlanta. And there also he met a girl from Rome, Georgia, named Sara Arnold. After a year he married her, and the two of them took every nickel they had and spent three wonderful months in Italy.

When they returned to Atlanta they were nearly broke. They found themselves a little apartment, bought a phonograph and some records, a pair of canaries and a maidenhair fern, the canaries and the fern because they could not face life in an apartment without reminders of the out-of-doors. There was a dime left, and this Athos used for carfare.

"While he was downtown," Sara Menaboni says, "I emptied the ice box, tossed together what I had, and made a lunch. And at noon Athos came back; I heard him laughing before he opened the door."

He had stopped to see four friends with whom he had worked, and found they had been unable to decide what to buy the Menabonis for a wedding present. So they gave Athos an envelope with four five-dollar bills in it. It was the beginning of the up-grade, a long and rather slow pull, but a steady one. The years in the apartment were followed by a period in a rented country house that ended when the owner cut down the trees and left the Menabonis' most important friends, the birds, homeless. Just at this time, the property that now is Valle Ombrosa came on the market, was bought, and plans for a house were made. These last were abandoned because of the late war, and a small house substituted that is a showplace, unique for the way in which it fits its uses, and its owners fit into it.

The house is literally a house the birds built, for in November 1938 Sara Menaboni, on impulse, persuaded her husband to make a light wooden carrying case and to send it, with 35 of his paintings inside, to a sister-in-law—Augusta Arnold of Ramsey, N. J.—with a letter asking Mrs. Arnold to see what could be done to call the pictures to the attention of New York.

Mrs. Arnold is a quite frank person, and admits that her first reaction was annoyance. Her second reaction was curiosity about her own ability to place the paintings before the public. Her third was to take the case, go to New York, and there to trudge from museum to gallery to decorator to what-not. What surprised her was that the moment the case was opened it invariably attracted excited and yet respectful consideration.

In a short time powerful friends were found at the American Museum of Natural History, the Audubon Society, the Kennedy Galleries—many other places. These friends found a great deal more than merely accurate representation in Menaboni's paintings. The painter had had experience in every medium open to the artist, and was familiar with all the techniques and unhampered by most of the difficulties that continuously beset his great prototype, Audubon. Many of his friends felt that there was a rhythmic quality, a vividness and a freshness about Menaboni's work that certainly had not been surpassed by his predecessors. They are, in a peculiar way, bird paintings for today that seem to appeal equally to everyone from the professional ornithologist to the man who sees them on the cover of a Sunday magazine. A number of them have appeared there, by the way, because of a long friendship between the Menabonis and Angus Perkerson, who edits the Sunday magazine of the Atlanta *Journal*.

Because there may be some reason for explaining how, on occasion, a book originates, let me say this book began purely through chance. Late in the winter of 1945 the writer passed through Atlanta at the fag end of a two-month trip to the Coast that had included a great many cities and for that matter, a great many people. One Sunday morning in an Atlanta hotel the boy brought up the Atlanta *Journal* and there, on the cover of the magazine, were two angry Blue Jays screaming at a little snake that was foolishly crawling up a twig. The picture seemed to me unique: out of a good many thousands of bird pictures I had seen this seemed to me the first that had any great quality of immediateness, or great quality of interest beyond accurate reproduction.

First there was a telephone call to Angus Perkerson, and then for two days there were calls to the Menabonis. And no answer. Back in New York letters were exchanged, and later still an agreement was reached. Athos's chief interest was in as nearly perfect reproduction as could be had in a fallible world; Sara's desire was to provide an informal accompanying text that would reflect as truly as possible the feeling as well as the fact which has supported the Menabonis in their joint interest—and passion.

There were many difficulties, some mechanical, some having to do with the abnormal difficulties of producing a beautiful book in a post-war morass of shortages, indifferent qualities, shocking price rises. These difficulties required five years' work to overcome, but in this long period a book that began as a commercial proposition has become a labor of love for some hundreds of people.

This, then, is the story of a little boy in Livorno who watched birds fly away, but who remembered the birds and learned well how to paint them for an audience he did not then know existed.

June, 1950   J. S.

CHAPTER ONE

{ *Valle Ombrosa*
Atlanta, Georgia
Summer, 1950 }

AT THE START, let me say that my husband and I do not slam doors shut; instead, we open them wide. This minute I am opening a new door for myself by starting to relate a way of living.

First, I have a difficulty to mention. The present is so filled with interest that I scarcely know how to buckle down to describing past experiences. For example, right now while I desire earnestly to concentrate upon writing, a baby gray squirrel, named Sussi, is in my lap, trying to claim my whole attention. He nibbles at my elbows, wanting me to play with him. He is turning somersaults—now scooting around in back of me—and he must think it is the height of pleasure to use my back as a race track. I shall put him in another room.

A second ago I scanned my notes and find that on June 30, 1941, I was in the same difficulty that I am at the present: "With so much happening constantly and unexpectedly how can I put my thoughts in a neat and orderly pattern? I follow one idea, then my thoughts flutter about as the butterfly I see before me now. There is so much I want to say, and my experiences, impressions, and interpretations pile up so high before me that I do not know how I can ever get them all down on paper before I forget them. I make a vow to start doing so, then something new claims my attention. Nature does not stand still, nor wait for laggards to catch up."

However, that June morning I kept on the woodland path, for I had the hope of finding an ideal state of mind for writing on the secluded island that was part of the property we were then renting. Determinedly, I had set out with a notebook and pencil to be materially equipped for the job. I thought that surely I could collect a great many ideas suitable to be put down on the inviting pages.

I pushed my way through mountain laurel and azalea to get to the island. True, it was a tiny island, but a charming place to hide from the world for a while. If I must be absolutely truthful about my retreat, the "island" was only a big rock in the stream, covered with a moss rug, green and, usually, dry and soft. However, that morning it was soggy from a recent shower. Being a woman, naturally I did not want to get wet, so I sat on the leather notebook that I had had the foresight to bring along.

My husband joined me. He saw the perfect setup for a joke at my expense. "I thought you were going to write. What weight you are giving to your pages!"

How could I write, when I had to concentrate upon a hooded warbler that came to look at me inquisitively? A red-eyed vireo joined him; then a splotchily colored male summer tanager. The three birds were less interested in me than I was in them, though, for shortly they flew away.

The summer tanager, varicolored because of the seasonal molt, decided to take a bath downstream twenty feet from me. Perhaps he wanted to show me that he could not help the fact that he was changing feathers and looked such a fright while doing so. Maybe he wanted to prove, too, that he had not been stained in dye pots. Although that was my fancy, I should probably be more realistic and say that perhaps his mites were bothering him and he hoped that a bath would rid him of the vermin.

A blue jay came to splash in the water, but the busybody could not take time for a decent bath. He had to hurry away in order not to miss anything going on elsewhere.

Two brilliant damsel flies came into sight—exquisite fairy airplanes with gossamer wings and streamlined shiny metallic bodies—and made gyroscopic landings on a green leaf field. As they opened and closed their wings, they seemed poised for a take-off at any moment.

A few minutes before, Athos had moved away from me but as I sat, watching the damsel flies in their mating, I heard him whistle to me. I knew that whistle to mean some extraordinary occurrence; and went swiftly from my island to join him.

He told me that he had heard the screeching of birds in the thicket, and at first thought that two males must be fighting, but a sharp outcry that soon followed had told him this was no mere quarrel. He had summoned me because he suspected that something desperately tragic was happening amid the thick bushes.

We started to run closer to the scene of action and caught a flash of red—cardinals! They were screaming frantically. And it was nesting season!

Athos dived into the thicket ahead of me, not thinking of caution. "A snake!" he called to me. "A black snake with a baby cardinal in its mouth! The head is already being swallowed!"

The next instant I saw him reach down for a handy stick, and faster than I can describe it he beat at the snake.

He called to me again, "I hit the tail, but the snake has got away. It dropped the little bird." He stooped, then straightened up, holding the young bird. "It seems lifeless."

Together we examined the bird that lay motionless in Athos's hand. No—it wiggled a little! The head was bleeding and the closed eyes were swollen and sticky with snake saliva. Fortunately we had read in the *Field Book of Snakes*, by Schmidt and Davis, that "snake's saliva retards or prevents coagulation of the blood," so immediately we took the foundling to the stream to wash it. After cleaning it, Athos wrapped it carefully in his handkerchief to keep it warm. Then we began searching for the nest that must be somewhere near by. We found it on a low dogwood branch—empty. The structure, which had been carefully built of twigs and rootlets and lined with fine grasses, was torn beyond the possibility of further use.

Upon hearing a faint squeak, my attention was called to another wee brownish creature perched on a low alder branch, and it, too, was gathered into protective hands. Still another fledgling chirped, giving the direction of its whereabouts to Athos. We looked but could find no others.

The adult birds were still flying about helplessly, screaming. With the nest torn up, the little ones too young to fly and one of them wounded, there was nothing we could do save adopt the three infants ourselves, no matter how much we regretted not restoring them to the care of their rightful parents; the odds were too unfavorable on the triplets' reaching maturity had we left them where they were.

At home, the wounded bird was wobbly on its legs and could not open its eyes, but the bleeding had ceased. In the days following, it recovered so completely that no trace was left of its narrow escape from death.

The little cardinals were fluffy balls of a color like their mother, but with horn-colored bills, not like the bright red of the female. Without tails they looked unfinished, yet already they had cocky miniature topknots that they raised or lowered at will. We could not determine their sex at that time.

Their most compelling feature was an incessant squeaking to be fed. At first we had to force-feed them by prying open their bills and poking the food down their throats with a small soft paint brush. But shortly they learned to open their bills whenever we approached them—three mouths flying open begging for food. Until they should be old enough to eat seeds, berries, and some insect matter, we had to work out a formula, and happily we chanced upon the right one—mashed hard-boiled egg, a few drops of olive oil, a teaspoonful

of raw oatmeal and one of wholewheat flour, bound together with enough water to make a soft paste. Occasionally we supplemented their diet with finely chopped raw meat, and as the food was thrust down their throats they gurgled contentedly.

They started flying short distances inside our screened porch, but without knowing where to land; one minute they would hit the wall and flutter down it to the floor, the next they would dive straight at our faces or into the screens. Soon they managed to make perfect landings on the branches that Athos attached securely on the porch wall for them, and found delight in hopping from one twig to another. They stretched and preened their feathers, squeaked for food, and dozed or slept with heads under wings.

Subconsciously they must have been concentrating hard upon growing tails, for the reddish feathers came out remarkably fast. Little by little other body feathers appeared in place of old ones shed, giving them a splotchily red coloration. With this evidence we knew that all three were males.

When they were fully able to fend for themselves, we liberated them. They stayed close about the house, eating at the feeding station or from our outstretched hands whenever we went outdoors. They seemed particularly fond of sunflower seeds.

During the winter our tame birds were a constant delight to us and to our visitors. It was a satisfaction to know that we had successfully reared them, and that they did not want to leave us. However, cardinals who have lived peaceably together during the winter still have strong feelings about territorial rights. It was inevitable that with the advent of the spring mating season, only one should remain, with the mate he had selected. Shortly after the other birds left, we discovered the nest of the remaining pair in a wild grapevine on the fence. We knew that we must not touch the four bluish-white eggs speckled with cinnamon-brown, but must hold a mirror over the nest to see the eggs inside.

We noted that when the female came to the feeding station, her husband chased her to a near-by perch, to wait for him to bring the seeds to place in her bill; he was determined to bring food to her and not to let her get it for herself. She fluttered her wings as she accepted his offerings. Many times a day when she was on the nest, he came to our outstretched hands for sunflower seeds to take to his lady.

After the eggs were hatched, the male was busier than ever with the responsibilities of fatherhood. Apparently he worked as hard to feed the brood as the female did. When the young birds learned to fly, he did not teach them to come to our hands for sunflower seeds, but he came oftener than before. Cardinal youngsters are not weaned from parental care for quite a long period, and having these eastern cardinals stay close about us suited us well.

It was particularly pleasant to hear the male singing in his clear, full voice; to listen to the calls of the female, and the chirping of the offspring as they followed their parents. Luckily our southern climate was such that these birds remained with us in winter instead of migrating farther south. We had fun speculating upon how many generations of cardinals would be in our woods, reproduced from this one male of the three we had saved from an untimely death. For the one brood was scarcely weaned when the female laid a second clutch of eggs. And so another life cycle began.

Now, this morning some years later, Athos is painting a cardinal picture. It is not for our eyes alone; many persons will see it.

Memories troop before my sight now and I find myself going back seven years to the time when we were living in an apartment in Atlanta, and to a turning point in our lives.

Athos had never painted a bird picture, although birds were nearly always to be found in his mural paintings—a kind of Menaboni hallmark to those familiar with his work. Quite casually one morning Athos said that he would paint a cardinal picture to be hung on our own wall.

Though I paid little attention to his remark, I did hear him say, "Americans do not fully appreciate the birds they have. The first time I saw a cardinal was in Florida, while driving through a lane with dense, dark vegetation on each side, and all of a sudden a male cardinal flew in front of the automobile. The sun shone on him, and I had a flash of red—like a flame!"

I observed that he was happily absorbed in his new experiment, and I was satisfied that he had something to occupy him pleasantly while waiting for another mural painting commission.

When I looked at the finished picture, I exclaimed, "How could you paint cardinals so accurately from memory?"

"You forget that ever since I discovered cardinals in Florida," Athos explained, "I have looked at them for years. I have wanted to see them at every opportunity and to see them in detail."

His memory had retained the living pictures of these birds. I, one of the Americans who did not fully appreciate birds, had seen them with half an eye, and therefore had retained nothing but a flash of red across my consciousness. Now my Italian-born husband had opened my eyes. Fra Lippo Lippi said:

We're made so, that we love
First, when we see them painted, things we have passed
Perhaps a hundred times, nor cared to see.

Cardinal

Later I was to learn that at my old home in Rome, Georgia, on one acre there was an abundance of songbirds that I have not since seen equaled on so small a plot of ground. My father had always loved, fed, and protected his birds. For twenty-one years I had lived in a veritable bird paradise, without caring to see the occupants, knowing that they were my friends, or being aware that they were to change the whole course of my life.

I confess that at the time I looked at that bird picture I saw the pair of cardinals only as pretty subjects for Athos, not as birds deserving in their own right to be studied, loved, and protected. Besides, I had no time to look long at that picture, for the afternoon it was finished and while the paint was still wet, an interior decorator came to see us. She saw the picture as decorative, functional art. She said, "It is exactly what a client of mine needs on her living-room wall. May I take it?" We reluctantly agreed to sell it.

I had an indefinable feeling that in parting with that picture Athos had let go something that was more precious to him than any creation of his past. It was as though there had been taken from him a first baby bird that had not grown feathers—a brain child that he would have liked to cherish himself, yet which had been snatched away from him, probably never to be seen again.

He had had such pleasure painting it, and still we did not have a bird picture to use in our home; so he started upon another bird subject. He was deeply in love with this new-found expression of his art. Indeed, when the second picture was finished, he immediately started upon a third, and I saw that painting birds was becoming an obsession with him. I had never seen him work so contentedly—no, that was too mild a description—he was so feverishly engrossed in his work that little else mattered to him in that period.

One day, with a sigh of resignation—even martyrdom—he said despondently, "I suppose that I must quit this painting of birds for my own pleasure, and hustle about town to find another mural commission. I can't play truant to workaday problems."

Ah, yes, the apartment rent had to be paid monthly, the dentist, the butcher, and the baker wouldn't wait forever. Selling one cardinal picture was not enough, and the weeks were passing quickly. But then I stopped to think: Athos had been living so richly while painting his favorite subjects that it was beyond thinking about that he should stop because of financial necessity. I have never hated the lack of money as I did at that moment.

Vehemently I declared, "To heck with money! You go on painting birds and enjoying yourself!"

Eagerly he caught up his pencil to start drawing a new bird subject, and was happy again. It was as though, now that he had unlocked a door for himself, no day was long enough for him to put down in paint what birds meant to him. I started economizing in every way, to make our shrinking bank account last as long as it could. If Athos was happy painting what he wanted most to paint, then it was up to his wife to provide him with the proper environment and frame of mind to do so. I would not slam shut a door through which he could pass to his new-found joy.

One of the things that pleases Athos is to be read aloud to while he works. We started with Peattie's life of John James Audubon, *Singing in the Wilderness*. Athos took unto himself every word, and it had a profound influence upon him. I took unto myself Lucy Audubon. I cried over her, not because of her self-sacrifice, the hardships she endured, and her assuming the responsibility of rearing the children; no, I cried because she was denied so many years of being with her husband while he tramped the forests alone or went from city to city, and even to England, soliciting subscriptions to the forthcoming publication of *The Birds of America*. I wept because she was denied the joys of being at her husband's side while he painted his masterpieces.

Following this, we read together a book of the life of the "poverello" of Assisi, St. Francis, who loved birds so fervently that never before or since has anyone equaled that ardor. The pages revealed the utmost in human dedication to nature.

Vaguely, yet surely, I was aware that something of prime importance was happening in our lives. Something better and stronger was stirring within us, inspiring us to new heights.

Our friends saw the growing collection of pictures and were unanimously enthusiastic about them. Furthermore, they entered eagerly into their making, bringing to us living birds and armfuls of flora from which Athos could select the plant he wanted to use as background material, even taking us in their automobiles out to the fields to study birds on the wing. In countless ways people entered into the bird pictures.

Every one of them was insistent that the collection be sent to a New York gallery. No one in Atlanta had another idea at that time of what other ways the pictures should, or could, be used.

Athos shrugged his shoulders hopelessly. He knew New York in the past: it was impossible for an unknown artist, in a new field of painting, to get anyone of authority even to look at his works. I thought it was tragically sad to be unknown, without the magic of an established name.

But I have always disliked that word "impossible." Let a thing be called impossible, and that

thing is going to be tackled and made a possibility. It was only a matter of opening the right door. Which door? If Athos's bird pictures had to be sold for our financial livelihood so that he might continue painting them, and an art gallery was what he needed, why, then those pictures would be placed in a gallery!

Let Athos go right on with the painting that gave him so much happiness, without giving another thought to other matters. My duty would be to think out the rest and carry through somehow. The big question was, How?

I made an ally of my brother's wife, Tommy, in New York. She wrote that she had been looking for some project that would be fun in which to get interested, and we had presented her with a stimulating one. She said that we would cope with all the impossibilities; and the word "cope" entered my vocabulary, to be used gleefully since. The whole affair was a lark.

The first week Tommy sent a telegram: "Whoops my dears the American Museum of Natural History wants an exhibition." The second week she telegraphed: "The National Audubon Society wants an exhibition." The third week she wired: "Kennedy Gallery wants an exhibition." We were off to a flying start.

This is not the time to record how everything was accomplished. Dozens of friends, dozens of strangers were anxious to help Athos in the project of painting the American birds. Before we could catch our breaths, there was more demand for bird pictures than Athos could supply. The matter of finances was amply taken care of and became an insignificant one, as it should be with a creative person—and as it was not with poor Audubon. In Athos's era it was disclosed that his love for birds was appreciated by others, and that his pictures fulfilled a deep need. In every way they could, people made it possible for him to continue painting the birds that they, too, loved.

A pair of cardinals first, then whole flocks of birds, had given to me and to many other persons wide vistas hitherto unseen, opening up a bright new world with its bountiful blessings.

The squirrel has now returned to climb all over me, being an adorable nuisance. Bless his little heart, he is so filled with the joy of living that he wants to include me in it. The other day Athos saw him outdoors, utterly helpless on the ground, while a coiled pilot black snake was constricting the life out of him. Needless to say, Athos restored Sussi to his place among the living.

Now I cannot ignore the fact that my attention is claimed by the insistent Present. Sussi is urging me to see that it is now time to fix his bottle.

We had spent the early part of last night at the home of a friend and, upon our return, I lingered on our terrace, reluctant to go inside to my bed; it was too perfect a moonlit September night to miss entirely.

I could not see the Shrine of St. Francis, in the shadows of the overhanging trailing rose, but I was strongly conscious of the presence of the Saint watching me as I stood bathed in the bright moonlight; the Patron Saint of all living creatures was not a mere statue upon the wall of our house, but a living saint. Those mystic, compelling eyes, which I could not see, were boring into my soul, trying to tell me something that mute lips could not. Was there something more that I must see, other than the beauty of the outlined trees, and the shadows, and the bright orb in the heavens?

Athos stood poised. Was he also waiting?

Suddenly the silence was pierced by a scream.

Instantly we knew by whom the shrill cry had been emitted. Late in the afternoon Athos had seen a baby squirrel, smaller than Sussi, upon a pine trunk, crying pitifully; however, when Athos had approached him he had scrambled up the trunk out of reach. How had he got out of his nest? Where was his mother? Was he the

Barn Swallow

brother of Sussi? What had forced him out alone into the world? These were questions that no person could answer. Out of the night the voice came to us telling us plainly that the baby was frightened, hungry, cold, helpless.

We discussed the possibility of finding the squirrel. It seemed a hopeless task. The animal could be anywhere among the hundreds of trees —high up in one of them—a minute creature in the bigness of the outdoors. Although the moon was bright, there was only shadow in the tree thicket, and our flashlight was out of commission. We were helpless to assist the helpless. The squirrel would die naturally or be the victim of some predator who could see in the night and climb or fly to the tree height where he was.

With sadness and impotency, we went inside the house. I wandered about aimlessly, loath to undress.

Again came the loud outcry—the squirrel was calling frantically. Was St. Francis, throwing his voice as a ventriloquist, telling us to try to save a life?

"I can't go to bed," I said to Athos. "We have to see if we can do something for that baby squirrel!"

He felt the same way. Before the words were out of my mouth, he was hunting a cloth with which to handle the wild creature, should he be able to catch the poor thing, for he knew from experience that untamed squirrels can bite hard.

As we went down the hill, we told each other that even if we could not see the squirrel, at least we were seeing the beauties of nature in the moonshine. I knew that this was small talk; there was nothing that we wanted to see save that lone squirrel.

In the thicket of trees we stopped, waiting for a sound to give us the location of the squirrel. There was a small sign—oh, blessed ears to assist the eyes—and our attention was drawn to a certain group of trees.

My husband's eyes are sharper than mine. "There he is!" he whispered, and pointed. "On the trunk of the second tree from us."

There was the outline of the little squirrel, flat against the trunk! He was just above hand reach, but perhaps he would come down—or would he be scared at seeing us and go higher?

Breathless, motionless, we waited Nothing happened.

Then Athos crept closer.

Instead of scurrying higher, the squirrel came down the trunk a foot; he was within reaching distance. Athos edged still closer, stopped, and both he and the squirrel made no movement for several minutes. Then, with a lunge, Athos pounced upon the squirrel. There was a scream from the squirrel and a call from Athos, "I've got him!"

I saw Athos's hands working with the cloth and knew that the squirrel must be trying to bite, but as we walked back to the house the squirrel quieted down and lay still in the cloth.

In the bright light of the room he blinked. He accepted our caresses without objection. I heated milk, diluted with water and sweetened with honey, and after the medicine dropper was in his mouth, he tasted the milk, found it good, and sucked eagerly. There was no way of knowing how long it had been since he had had a meal; certainly his teeth were not strong enough to gnaw nutshells.

With his tummy full, it was time that he get to sleep. In the basket under the covering was Sussi curled up. We uncovered him and introduced him to Biribissi. (A favorite book for children in Italy has the title *Sussi and Biribissi.*) Biribissi nestled close to his brother and we saw something that I shall never forget; Sussi kissed the new fellow all over. Then we tucked them in for the night and they settled contentedly to rest.

I felt that St. Francis must be resting serenely in his shrine; we had heeded his message, and he had given us the eyesight to see what he had wanted us to see.

William Hamilton Gibson in *Sharp Eyes* wrote: "It matters not in what particular direction the eye is educated; the habit of observation in one field quickens the powers of perception in any other, and the results depend not upon the eye—the camera—but upon the spirit and inspiration behind the retina, for 'there is no more power *to see* in the eye itself than in any other jelly'; in the words of William Blake, 'we see *through* it, not with it,' even as through our spectacles."

And now I see two furry little heads with great black eyes peering at me from over the edge of their basket. Who says that creatures of nature cannot talk? Their attitudes tell me that it is time to give Sussi and Biribissi their second feeding of the morning.

15

Least Tern

CHAPTER TWO

I LET THE FORCES of nature take charge of me this morning. For a time I sat at the belvedere that commands a fine prospect of the hills and the valley, recalling a morning in early summer when Athos and I had been breakfasting at this same spot. I had had a mighty urge to see ALL and take unto myself everything that nature offered to me. I had cast my eyes into the high places.

What was that tiny movement in the top of a sweet gum tree? I concentrated upon it. A hummingbird was circling among the tall branches! Why that peculiar behavior? I watched, breathless.

The hummingbird alighted upon a branch and preened its feathers. I told Athos where to find the minute bird with his eyes and, while he watched the bird at rest, I ran indoors to fetch the field glasses.

Upon my return I focused the powerful lens upon the bird, which was still at its task of preening. I identified it as a female. Then she moved, and I followed her a foot distant as she alighted upon the side of her wee nest! It was well over a hundred feet high in the trees, although ruby-throated hummingbird nests are usually found only fifteen to twenty-five feet up.

I had never seen a hummingbird upon her nest. Indigenous only to this continent, of all places in eastern North America that she could have selected for her nesting site she had come directly to us. I had at last seen what I wanted to see by casting my eyes to high places.

Nor was the sight a momentary pleasure, for the female apparently had not yet laid her two white eggs, and for weeks, through the glasses, I could see her every day in her bower. From below I could not see her feeding her babies, but I could imagine the sight. And when she came to feed many times a day upon the flowers about our house, how glad we were that we had provided her with flowers specially planted to attract hummingbirds; we had gone a step further by providing a glass tube, especially blown for hummingbird feeding, containing sugared water.

The drive of the wings is so fast that human eyes cannot see the upstrokes and downstrokes, but only a blur such as an airplane propeller makes in motion. The hummingbird's unsurpassed skill in control, to "stand still" in the air or fly backwards, is a marvel to behold. Contrary to popular opinion, this is not the only bird able to perform these two feats, although none is capable of sustaining himself as long as the hummer. We have seen kingfishers stand still in the air over water before diving for fish; and watched terns, also over water, after spotting fish that they had overlooked, with a few backward strokes of their wings retrace their course to be perpendicular to their prey, stand still a few seconds, and then dive. However, according to our observations, the hummingbird is unique in his ability to fly sideways, as though swinging in mid-air. This is a common performance during the fighting of two hummingbirds.

I remember once, years ago, a man clad in overalls had appeared at my door. For a moment I had had a fleeting and unkind thought: What is this stranger here to get from me?

"Are you Mrs. Menaboni?" he asked shyly.

As I answered, I wondered how he knew my name.

"You wrote in the newspaper yesterday that you had never seen a hummingbird nest close up. I have come fifteen miles to bring one to you that I found last winter."

The man had brought to me the best gift within his power. He held for my inspection a small crotched limb, with a hummingbird nest saddled upon it. Cup-shaped, covered externally with lichens fastened with spiderwebs, inside it was made of the finest of plant down. In size the delicate structure was only one and a half inches in diameter; the hollow only three-fourths of an inch, suitable for the tiniest of fledglings.

I was so overcome with emotion that words almost failed me. The least I could do was to offer him the hospitality of my home. I invited him to come inside the living room, called Athos to share the present the man had given, and, together, we entertained him as an honored guest.

Later we paid him a visit at his home. He was an ardent bird lover and there were no barriers between us, for we had a mutual interest.

One evening a couple we did not know came to us. The man held a jewelry box in his hand, and gave it to us. Athos opened it, and reposing upon white cotton were dazzling rubies, gleaming emeralds, and jet—not cold, inert stones—living jewels!

Lying limp in the box was a male ruby-throated hummingbird, a little over three inches in length. The couple had found him almost dead through exposure to the sudden and unseasonably cold weather. They had brought the begemmed bird to us, for they had heard that we knew how to care for birds. They brought more—the beginning of a lasting friendship.

The hummingbird knew, in some occult manner, that we would not harm him, but would help him in his time of need; trustingly he perched upon Athos's finger, and gratefully he sipped with his long tongue from the glass tube the proffered sugared water. Our new friends sighed with relief that they had brought their foundling to the proper home.

The next day, after remembering that I had seen a photograph of a hummingbird hovering in the air in front of gladioli, and thinking that our new little guest might like gladioli nectar better than artificial food, I purchased a bouquet

of the flowers to bring to him. But he was an odd creature! He never once explored with his long tongue the possibility of juice in the flowers, but he did see a certain bent stem of a gladiolus that suited him ideally as a perch. After a week, when the dead flowers had dropped off, the humming-bird still preferred his resting place on the bent stem to all other perches in our house. I did not have the heart to throw out the ugly remnants of the once-lovely flowers, until we were expecting visitors who would see only that there were shriveled stems in the vase.

We put the hummingbird in the screened porch, and he could not find a perch that suited him. After Athos brought indoors a selected small branch to attach to the wall of the porch, the midget decided that it was what he had been hunting for in his new living quarters. He spent much of his time on his perch, preening his feathers and looking about him.

But we did not know that we were giving our hummingbird an incomplete diet, until one night we left the porch light burning and the bird showed us that he had to have a great quantity of small insects to eat as well as honeyed or sugared water. From that time forward we turned on the porch light every night, to attract innumerable insects screened to the right size for our wee guest.

Nor did it occur to us that he might like a bath, until the windy day that rain fell on the tiled floor of the porch, and the hummer took a thorough bath in a puddle. We gave him a saucer, constantly filled with a quarter-inch of water, and from that day, each morning at a definite time, he hopped gleefully into his bathtub.

However, we did see when the time had come to liberate the little fellow, to live in his natural environment. We wanted him to get to the peak of physical strength before autumn came, when he would make his long migratory flight. He had to go to warmer climes for the winter months, to southern Florida, or perhaps even to Central

18

America, and be able to make the amazing non-stop flight across the five hundred miles of the Gulf of Mexico.

He rode outdoors on Athos's finger, clinging to it with his diminutive feet. For a time he looked about him, taking in the scene. After this hesitation, he flew a few feet to a low dogwood limb and busily preened his feathers. Then he decided to reconnoiter a bit, circled the house, and returned to his dogwood limb for further preening and gazing about him. Lastly, with the swiftness of lightning, he zoomed beyond the limits of our sight.

He was not lost to our sight forever, for we knew that with another summer our living jewels would return to us.

Oliver Wendell Holmes has put it: "Those who are really awake to the sights and sounds which the procession of the months offers them, find endless entertainment and instruction. Yet there are great multitudes who are present at as many as three score and ten performances, without ever really looking at the scenery, or listening to the music, or observing the chief actors."

One time Athos and I were at Pine Mountain Inn in central Georgia, and, at sunset, had our dinner on the terrace overlooking the valley. We selected a table by the balustrade in order to see to best advantage the magnificent scene below us. The music started: a sparrow hawk came calling "killy-killy-killy," as though strolling across the stage singing to himself, unmindful of an audience. From the opposite direction, the next actor came squeaking upon the stage, a belligerent hummingbird, who had spied the hawk intruding upon his territory. For fully ten minutes we witnessed the fearless hummingbird chase the sparrow hawk (many times his size) around in circles. The hawk was given a miserable time, although he endeavored in vain to fight back and kept up his cry of "killy-killy-killy" unceasingly. In our opinion, the hummingbird could not do any injury to the hawk, but could, through

superior flying ability, annoy him to distraction, just as a buzzing fly sometimes annoys us to near madness. Finally the hawk had had quite enough, and left the scene quickly, admitting defeat. Satisfied that he had conquered, the lilliputian warrior turned around to disappear from whence he had come. No other person on the terrace had been aware of the highly entertaining and instructive performance.

There is no way of knowing in advance what delights are in store for us outdoors. The other day Athos was using the water hose to fill a large concrete basin inside the aviary. Instead of waiting until his tub was filled, the golden eagle decided that he would take a shower bath. He ruffled up his feathers, shook himself, and turned to wet his back, keeping wide open his seven feet of wings.

Then Athos heard the unmistakable squeak of a hummingbird near by. He turned his head to see that the minute bird had filtered through the wire into the cage, and, hovering, was studying the water spray. The sun rays were at the proper angle on the hummingbird's throat to make it scintillate metallic red. That in itself was enough to make the scene memorable for Athos.

Athos then witnessed what probably no other person has seen or in all likelihood will ever see: while one of our largest birds was taking his shower, the smallest of our birds darted into and out of the water a dozen times, often within ten inches of the eagle, until, finally, the hummingbird was so wet that he had some difficulty in flying outside the cage to a limb upon which to sun-bathe and preen his feathers.

Can it be only seven years since my eyes were opened to the new world of nature—open to such a wideness that I am afraid I shall miss some wonderful experience—yes, and fulfillment—if I do not live from moment to moment?

Knowing that there must be a background of past experiences to educate the individual

he guided by St. Francis to come straight to us for a purpose? I was no longer superficially amused; I looked at that bird with a profound respect, even bordering upon reverence. He was the beginning of my own interest in birds.

The appearance of the coot was striking. The velvety black head and neck were soft and sleek, reminding me of sealskin; and the rest of his feathers were beautiful blendings of slate-gray, with a touch of white on each wing. His legs and ridiculously large feet were olive-green. There were dark wine-colored markings on the ivory bill. And, as though Nature had wanted to give him a dash of bright color to relieve his somberness, he had ruby-colored eyes.

His lobed feet, with toes having scalloped flaps, indicated that he was a river, lake, and marsh bird. The oversized feet would keep him from sinking in soft ooze, besides aiding him to be a fine swimmer. In the apartment his feet made a clack-clacking on the hard floor. Because of those ludicrous feet, he has been called the "clown" among birds. Yet to me the coot was not a funny bird, for I could not disregard his solemn and melancholy expression.

Endeavoring to make him feel more at home, we filled the bathtub so that he could have a refreshing swim. He seemed to enjoy it, although he could not understand the slick enamel of the tub, which made climbing out of the water impossible when he wanted to leave it. We had to assist him from his bath.

He had quickly become accustomed to hands. In the afternoon a boy had cornered him in a pond so small that it was impossible for the bird to make a quick take-off; or maybe his little wings had been very tired after traveling a great distance. The son of one of our friends had held him while he telephoned to us that he had a "marsh hen." When we had arrived in the country to get the coot, there had been more handling. But the hands had been kind; they had not hurt him.

to emotional maturity, it would be unfair, ungrateful, and unwise not to pause often to consider the particular birds that wrought such a change in me, so I shall go back to those days when we lived in a city apartment, giving the basis upon which this very day is built.

To have so odd a bird as a coot share our few rooms was novel and amusing to me, though natural to Athos, whose youth in Italy had been occupied with strange creatures. However, to the American coot, belonging to the rail tribe of birds, we were the ones who must have appeared "as silly as a coot" to be living in such artificial, cramped quarters when there was the great outdoors to be lived in naturally.

Indeed, he must have felt definitely out of place in the small city apartment. It was strange enough for him to be inland as far as Atlanta, where there is scarcely enough water to attract coots. What quirk of nature had brought him to Atlanta? To see the beautiful homes, breathe the smoke, sip the famous cola drink? Or was

American Kestrel

The coot did not appear frightened or wild as he walked around examining our living room. It soon bored him, and he decided to go to bed under the sofa. He proved to be a nightwalker, however, and we heard him walking about in our bedroom several times, with his big feet making a clattering on the floor. We had read that coots were noisy birds, but aside from this he did not make a sound.

The bird liked to get under a chair or table and squat down quietly with his own coot thoughts. He was annoyed that Athos wanted him to pose for a portrait and, whenever approached, he would back off, making a motion as though to peck Athos, but after being held he was tranquil again and relaxed. His eyes were sad and his expression pensive always.

No matter how much we tried to coax and tempt him, the coot would not eat. We even put his food under water, thinking that he might like it that way, but he obstinately refused it. We decided to release him before he should get too weak from lack of food.

Late in the afternoon we took him to a near-by park and put him on the ground beside the lake. Strangely, something went wrong with his reasoning at that moment, for he ran as fast as he could in the opposite direction—right toward the road with the speeding automobiles! Athos chased after him, and fortunately had him safe in hand before a car wheel could get him.

Then Athos literally threw the coot into the water. In his element, he paddled his feet so fast that soon he reached the tiny island in the middle of the lake. He disappeared among the thick bushes there and, although we lingered to see how he would get along, stayed in hiding. Perhaps he wanted to get his bearings before attempting to fly away from the queer habitations of people.

We returned to our apartment. I kept remembering the way that bird had looked at *me* as the one who was "as silly as a coot" to be living

cooped up. *He* was once again "free as a bird."

In painting birds, Athos had newly found how he could be mentally as free as the birds. His world had expanded; mine was still restricted. Or was my narrow little world expanding, when a coot could show me that there was a whole great world for the taking if I did not let limitations restrict me?

Our next guest was very different. Not only appearance, instincts, and living habits were unlike those of the coot, his personality and mode of adaptation to his new environment were dissimilar. It is fun to have birds of marked contrasts, and fortunately I felt this way about the birds that came to us, for I was to find out that birds of many species would appear when least expected.

The newcomer was a southern screech owl, one of the smallest of the owls. His rufous coloration excited my curiosity, for I wanted to know why some screech owls were reddish, as ours was, while others from the same nest could be either rufous or gray. I could not know the answer to the dichromatic question, but I could observe the characteristics and behavior of a screech owl in an apartment.

And I could humor two of my friends who insisted that his name be Joe. For what reasons I have never ascertained, but if they wanted him to be Joe, Joe it would be!

After being taken from the box in which he had been brought to us, he blinked his greenish-yellow eyes in the bright light. Protesting, little Joe snapped his bill in castanet fashion. He had been caught in a rabbit trap earlier in the day, so that at least he must have felt relieved to be out of close confinement. Oh, I hoped that he would like his new home!

As soon as he spied a perch on top of the artists's easel, he flew from Athos's hand. He passed me in noiseless flight and, had I not seen him, I should have been conscious only of a slight breeze. Safely at a distance, he watched the people below with keen interest. He did not appear to bat an eyelid. He moved his head to follow the movements of his hosts, and at times we thought that he would surely screw his head off as he turned it right around to the back.

I hurried out to a market to buy meat and to beg some chicken feathers to mix with the meat, since from his Italian days Athos knew the owl needed a certain amount of indigestible matter that would later be ejected in matted round pellets. Not having had food all day, nor possibly the night before, Joe had a greedy appetite and ate out of our hands. We left food on a table for him to find during his night prowling.

We were pleased that he did not make the mournful, quivering cry in the darkness that one hears him make in the woods, not because we considered the sound to be one of ill omen, but because we could not associate a plaintive wailing with our new happiness in having such a guest. Indeed, the entire time he remained with us he was quiet. But all during these past years, whenever we have heard the unmistakable call of a screech owl, it has pleased us to associate it with that toylike Joe.

The first morning we had difficulty in locating him, for he had found a dark, secluded place to sleep behind a curtain. We did not disturb him until late in the day. His behavior led us to believe that he did not object to being handled; actually, he showed some signs of enjoying being stroked on the head. When we held him on our hands he seemed to be content there, although he could have flown away quickly, as another bird would have done. We were impressed by his gentle, docile disposition, and, in time to come, we were to use what we knew of Joe as a yardstick to measure the many screech owls that came to us and who never quite achieved his perfection as a pet. In this way we learned of the individuality of each bird within the same species.

Joe would sit still for hours. Occasionally he fluffed out his rust-red feathers to become quite round, and opened his eyes wide. Then, again, when alarmed, he elongated himself by pulling his feathers close to his body as he stood up straight, and his eyes were inconspicuous slits in his face; no doubt in his natural environment he thus looked like a broken branch of a tree. He raised or lowered his ear tufts at will, and his eyes had the same expression as those of a cat. I liked him best when he was sitting atop the easel, with his ear tufts raised, looking much like a fluffy kitten.

A visitor would not be aware of the presence of the owl in the studio for a long time. When he did catch sight of Joe, he would be fascinated by the direct glassy stare, although he would say nothing about what he saw and we would suppress our amusement. Finally the visitor would ask, "Is that a stuffed thing up on the easel?"

Even after we said that the "thing" was a living owl, some time would elapse before the visitor was convinced—not until he walked around the room and saw the owl eyes following him.

Then the visitor would ask, "Why do you have a thing like that in your apartment? It gives me the shivers!" For, invariably, the person had the usual childhood superstititions about owls. However, when we put Joe on the visitor's hand, and the pet behaved admirably while being stroked, the person would find pleasure in fondling the pretty creature. Joe made many friends, who went forth championing the cause of owls.

After Joe had lived with us for two months, and Athos had painted a picture of him, we decided that he should have his freedom. We let him go not because he seemed unhappy, but so that he might live in his natural habitat instead of in an artificial one. Athos opened a window screen at dusk, and held Joe outside in the air.

Joe had grown so accustomed to living with us that he appeared uninterested in the outdoors; he watched us with questioning eyes. Athos waved his hand up and down, trying to dislodge the bird, only to have him continue to cling to the hand he knew so intimately. It satisfied our vanity to know that he was reluctant to leave us.

After fifteen minutes of coaxing, Athos threw him into the air with a jerk, forcing him to fly. With a few flaps of his wings, and a gliding motion, Joe flew to a near-by chimney. We observed him through field glasses. He surveyed his surroundings, and soon afterward began preening his neglected feathers to get them in perfect condition. As night descended in earnest and our vision was dimmed, we caught our last glimpse of Joe still preening his feathers.

I wondered what thoughts of liberty he had and what degree of happiness he felt at being free again. How long would he retain a memory of his adventures? I hoped that he would not forget us, although I knew that it is a human conceit to wish to be remembered by those we love. And I admit openly that I had become sentimentally attached to Joe.

Nor was I the only one who had sentiment about Joe. The two friends who had named him saw his portrait and wanted to own it. To this day Joe, trapped symbolically in paint, "lives" with them. Athos and I visit him often in their home, and we, too, feel, as they do, that at any minute Joe will move on his tree perch.

Although Athos does not express himself verbally on the subject, there is a twinkle in his eyes and I fancy that he is suppressing a chuckle of exultation. He set the living Joe free, but he kept him alive in paint; Athos had eaten his cake and had it too.

One day we heard an eerie sound in the apartment building hall. Athos looked at me significantly, as he said, "I don't know who's coming, or what the person has, but I am sure that some sort of bird is being brought to us." Before the doorbell rang, Athos opened the door. The same friend who had brought Joe to us stood in the doorway holding a large crude cage.

"I don't know if you want a barn owl or not," she said dubiously.

"Decidedly I do," Athos greeted her. We did not know at that time what we were getting into.

The first impression we had of the barn owl was that his big, heart-shaped face resembled that of a monkey, which is the reason why he is often called the "monkey-faced owl." Set in white furry feathers, but circled by narrow reddish-brown ones, were big, oblique, brownish-black eyes. At the lower part of the white heart was the hooked bill, which looked like a blanched almond stuck there.

His general color was in shades of yellowish buff, speckled with black and white; his underparts were lighter colored with black dots. The feathers appeared very soft. He stood on long legs covered with hairy, pale-buff feathers and his powerful, scaly feet had dark, long talons.

It is usually difficult to measure such a term as "wrath"; before us stood about eighteen inches of it. As his fury increased, the barn owl lay down on his back with his legs and feet in the air making it threateningly obvious that he was ready to attack with his vicious talons anyone who dared to get close to him.

After some time he got on his feet again, lowered his head to the bottom of the cage, and swayed it sideways in the manner of a polar bear.

"Only a mother could love him," I quoted.

"He is an old bird and could not be easily tamed," Athos thought aloud. "Besides, turning him loose here would be like having a bull in a china shop. We must keep him caged until we free him."

Athos started drawing the owl, although it was a difficult job to observe him. Every time Athos approached the cage for a close view of the model, the furious bird lay on his back brandish-

Hooded Warbler

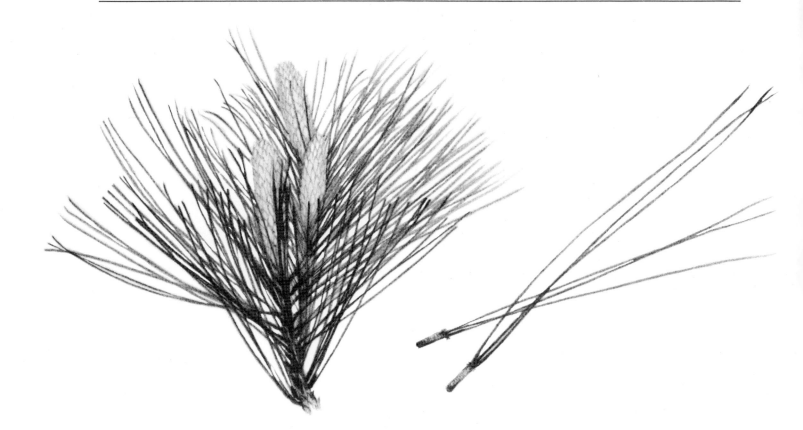

ing his claws, or else he humped over, with his head incessantly wagging from side to side. It was disconcerting, to put it mildly—and, in truth, there was nothing mild about that barn owl.

The worst soon started, and I shall carry the memory of it to my grave. He startled us with a cry that was a piercing, snakelike hiss, or perhaps it could be described as the kind of unnerving whistle that comes from a leaking radiator valve. Still, that was as nothing compared with the unholy sound that came at the end of the prolonged hiss, after we were sure he must be out of breath. This sound, if such a sound can be imagined, was like that of a baby being murdered.

Perhaps we could have recovered from the shock of such a gruesome noise once, but we had to endure it continuously all night. That blood-curdling sound continued relentlessly for three days and three nights, until we were ready to scream in the same ghastly manner. His fear-

some threatening to tear our flesh had had no effect, but the barn owl had found a better weapon to use against us.

Then I could well understand why barn owls had caused superstition and dread among people —a dread that still persists—though we know today that they help keep the balance of nature by eating enormous quantities of rodents, other small animals, and a few birds. This creature did not belong in a city apartment; he should have had a haunted house or a ghostly ruin from which to set out on his nightly killing ventures.

At evening three days later we summoned our friend to witness the liberation of the bird she had brought to us.

Athos placed the cage near the open bedroom window. For a time the owl did not notice that the door of the cage was open, he was so intent upon glaring at us. Then he stepped out on the window sill.

The sinister way in which the owl looked at us filled my friend and me with panic; we thought that any moment the owl would dash at us to claw out our eyes! She and I grabbed the bed covering to put over our heads, and Athos whooped with laughter.

We peeped from the cover in time to see the owl slide out the window into the air. Then, full of bravery again, we rushed to the window to watch him in flight. A more magnificent sight I have never seen. His wingspread must have been about forty-five inches, much greater than I had imagined, and when he languidly flapped his wings, they were like two waving feather fans. The owl glided silently in the direction of the park, and in the deepening twilight was lost to sight.

I forgave him for what we had been through, for superimposed over the memory of his horrible cry was a sublime memory—a memory so stamped upon my mind that, even now, I have only to close my eyes and I see the bird, wings spread, a huge, splendid moth.

October, and the pokeberries are ripe. A few minutes ago I saw Athos put a cluster of the berries inside the cage of the rose-breasted grosbeak, and I was reminded of the time we got him. He was one of the first native birds we had in our apartment. In fact, at that time Athos had not yet got federal and state permits to keep migratory birds in captivity.

We put the bird in a cage and he immediately took a long drink from the water cup. The magenta stain from the pokeberries that he had been eating when we chanced upon him in the woods was washed off his almost-white bill. The color of his bill had looked peculiar to us. It did not blend with the rose-red of the triangle on his breast or under his wings and it was small wonder that, at first, we had not known that he was a rose-breasted grosbeak. But for him the pokeberries had served as both food and drink, since he could not fly with a broken wing. They had been a lifesaver after the bird had been

shot, probably by a boy with a small gun. We brought a cluster of the berries to the apartment for him, but he must have been sick of the sight of them, for he would not touch one. In the cage we also put a bountiful supply of seeds which were more to his taste, and for dessert he found a slice of apple agreeable to his palate.

As we hovered over the cage, admiring his exquisite coloration, he cocked his head to look at us. He did not flutter about or show other signs of being afraid of us, and when Athos put his hand inside the cage to grasp him the grosbeak squatted down resignedly. While Athos tied the wing so that it would not droop, the grosbeak patiently suffered himself to be handled; he seemed to sense that Athos was doing all he could to aid him.

Our intention was to let the wing heal, then release the bird to continue his migration south. In the meantime Athos could paint his portrait. But when the time came for him to try his wings, we saw with sorrow that the broken bones had not set properly and knew that the grosbeak could never fly higher than a couple of feet.

One day our friend the federal judge came to see us and Athos confessed outright to him. "Judge," he said, "I am breaking the United States law," and proceeded to relate the history of the grosbeak in our possession. "What am I to do?" he asked.

The judge considered a moment, then pronounced seriously, "Athos, I sentence you to give the bird the best possible care for the rest of his natural life."

Since Athos is under sentence by a federal judge, the judge himself comes often to check up on the welfare of the bird that is our responsibility. For seven years we have given the grosbeak the best possible care.

In the apartment, I remember, we put him into a large cage with other birds to keep him company. Athos arranged a perch that enabled him to hop more easily to higher places, since he could not fly from the bottom of the cage to the top. He especially liked one fork in the branches. There he deposited his shelled nuts while eating them. He proved to be a perfect gentleman in all things, showing the utmost consideration to the foreign birds that shared his lodging. In fact, he was so kind and well mannered that often the other, more aggressive birds took advantage of him. But he never lost his good disposition.

There was one exceedingly vexing thing the grosbeak endured, which would have driven any other bird to distraction. One day, from out of the sky, an escaped chartreuse-colored parakeet came to our apartment-window feeding shelf. Athos had no difficulty in luring him indoors. (From where he had come we never knew. Fortunately for him, we alone, of all the thirty-six apartments in the building, had a window feeding shelf). The parakeet had been so accustomed to cage life that he immediately found the open door of our cage and made himself at home in it. Apparently he had to kiss and chatter all day with someone, so he tried every bird in the cage. None of them would have anything to do with the parakeet until he tried the grosbeak.

The parakeet made love to the grosbeak as though it were natural for him to do so. The fact that both were males made no difference to the parakeet. The grosbeak would move away, be persistently followed, until, out of weariness, he would accept the silly caresses. He could hardly eat, for the parakeet would be worrying him, and it took him a long time at night to get settled, because the parakeet would keep up his kissing.

We felt so sorry for the grosbeak's having to undergo such foolishness that we bought a lady blue parakeet. What fickleness! At once the chartreuse parakeet abandoned the grosbeak for his blue lady, to the grosbeak's obvious relief.

With the coming of spring, we heard soft tones from the cage. We had to look intently at the grosbeak to see his slightly parted bill and the quivering of his throat, but as we listened to his varied melody we could not remember having heard lovelier tones. Soon he took courage and his song rang out in its full glory. I do not know if he saw or heard any of his brothers migrating north. Perhaps he sang in the hope of attracting a mate. We always wondered if the grosbeak sang from instinctive urge alone or if he sang to keep up his morale. Year after year he sang at springtime.

This past year we made a valiant effort to help him secure a mate. Daily we hung his cage on a low branch of a tulip tree. One day his singing brought him a female, and he was in ecstasy. Athos used all his knowledge of trapping birds but, although the lady liked the grosbeak enough to stay about him for three days, she distrusted the trap and would not go near it. Finally she abandoned the male that would not come out in the open to court her, and went off with the other grosbeaks that were in flocks all about us. I felt terribly sorry that our grosbeak must be left without a lover. But then, I thought, perhaps it was all for the best, for if the female had been caught, no doubt I should have felt sorry about her lifelong confinement. Most of all I felt sad about the fate of our grosbeak, doomed to live his life alone despite the best of care.

It can do this particular bird no good, but, using him as an example, I have told and retold his story to boys, in the hope that it will persuade them not to use living birds as targets for their guns. Little boys do not seem to be impressed when told that it is against the law to shoot songbirds. It does seem to impress them when told that it is lots more fun to "shoot" birds with a camera, and at the same time develop a love and sympathy for them.

At this moment I hear a free grosbeak in my woods—hear his unmistakable clicking "tsck"— and I see my handicapped bird placidly eating his pokeberries. Close to his cage is another bird, of whom I shall write later, who loves him devotedly. Possibly the grosbeak finds some comfort in this fact and it makes his life more endurable. Although he does not demonstrate to Charlotte that he cares for her, I do know that he is a gentleman and deals with her in a gentle, considerate manner.

With no objective in mind—only for the pure pleasure of it—we have been walking in the rain this morning. I do not remember ever having gone walking in the rain while living in the apartment. There was no inspiration to be found on city sidewalks, under dripping eaves, beside automobiles splashing the unwary pedestrian with filthy water; nor was there much to see, save miserable human nature at its worst. However, this October morning we escaped from the comparative gloom of the house out to the dripping woods, where our spirits were filled with sunshine.

Had I not gone out I should not have seen the female rose-breasted grosbeak, nor the yellow-billed cuckoo, commonly called "rain crow," nor the fifty or sixty wood thrushes eating the dogwood berries; nor would I have seen the freak, single redbud blossom standing out in its lavender exclamation point. How cozy to be comfortably clad, so that only my face would get wet and to have on no cosmetics that would streak! How good to feel my sluggish muscles respond to action, making me tingle with vigor! How free I had become that I could sing at the top of my voice "Singing in the Rain" and know that nobody could say I was crazy! Streaks of rain made exclamation points that filled me with ideas ending in exclamation points!

Upon my return I saw Zulu huddled in his blanket on the sofa, and I felt sorry that his days of going out were over. Formerly, on such mornings as this, he rode papoose-like under my jacket, his walnut-sized head peeking out at the nape of my neck, his eyes peering at all the things outdoors. Although he is a marmoset, he

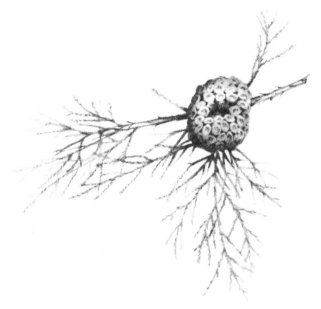

used to play very much like the baby squirrels, who are now about his adult size. His amber eyes are still bright, and he watches Sussi and Biribissi race about the sofa as he formerly did.

We have never been able to learn how long marmosets live. Zulu is a "common, or squirrel, marmoset" from tropical America, who by devious ways reached Atlanta when he was about a year or two old. He has been a part of our family for fifteen years, and only now shows signs of old age. A zoo director told us recently that perhaps Zulu is living a record number of years in captivity, for, in that particular zoo, marmosets had never lived more than about five years, because of the lack of freedom and the necessity for constant affection. Ours has been treated as an individual in our household—a personality that hundreds of persons have paid homage to—and when he passes on to the heaven of the monkeys we shall not be the only ones who grieve over the loss. May this not be soon!

We have found it interesting to watch how various animals and birds get along together. One of the things we shall never forget has taken place every winter morning for the past couple of years. In front of the open fire, on the warm hearth, Zulu would be stretched out full length, enjoying the heat; two inches from him would be sitting the Florida ground dove. Two inches from either of them would be the nose of the Irish setter who would be stretched full length on the rug. Our mischievous English sparrow would hop first to pull the tail of Zulu to make him scold, then to the ground dove to make her scold, then yank the whiskers of the dog to make him blink his eyes. Each of them tolerated the sparrow because they knew that the bird was merely playing. Athos and I would toast our toes as we ate our breakfast in front of the fire with the happy members of our family. We knew from pleasant experience that birds and animals and human beings could live together in accord.

I go back, for a moment, in memory to the first year that Athos and I had many native birds living with us in the apartment. It was remarkable that none of our birds objected to the tiny marmoset sitting in the sun atop their cage, not even when he entered through the open door to nibble at their fruits and shelled nuts or scatter the warbler's special food. They all accepted this smallest of monkeys as one of the household.

We had a petit hooded warbler, garbed in fine yellow, black, and olive feathers, who did his best to rival the grosbeak in song. We could have set our clocks by the regularity with which the warbler came out on the window sill every morning to take his bath. Afterwards he twitched his tail nervously, showing the white on it, and returned to the cage to shake himself dry before beginning his next singing performance.

One afternoon the warbler walked about on the rug, paying no attention to Zulu, who also was there. A devilish impulse prompted the marmoset to grab the warbler's tail. The bird squeaked shrilly and pulled away, leaving his tail feathers in the wee hands of the puzzled marmoset. We watched to see if the warbler would be frightened or resentful the next time the marmoset got near him. Although the bird continued to regard Zulu in the same casual, unconcerned manner as he had before the pluck-

ing, nevertheless, whenever the two were on the floor after that the warbler always faced Zulu, instead of turning his back trustingly.

We had at the same period three baby birds who reacted differently to the marmoset, and by so doing gave us a key to their individual characters. The fluff-ball, red-eyed towhee had no spirit, and was cowed by Zulu. The blue jay resented the marmoset's slapping him at mealtime, and would peck at the animal that was eating his egg mixture; but each knew exactly how far to go with the other. The strong-willed starling, in no uncertain terms, made the marmoset realize that at mealtime he was not to be disturbed by any monkey-business. This starling was the only bird ever to bully the marmoset.

Of course, at the time when we had Joe, the screech owl, visiting us, we couldn't leave him free in the same room with Zulu. If we had, there would have been no marmoset alive today, for Joe looked upon Zulu as merely a tasty morsel, the right size for a screech owl's meal. That was natural in a bird of prey, and strangely enough, Zulu did not seem to realize it, for he had no fear of Joe. Undoubtedly Zulu relied upon us for protection, and he delighted in deliberately teasing Joe.

For that matter, Zulu has never been afraid of anyone—not even of the starling—whom he deigned to respect merely at mealtime. Once we saw him jump on the back of a cat—scaring it out of one of its nine lives—and once he bit a strange dog that a visitor had brought into our house. He simply did not like dogs. Nor in late years will he tolerate monkey-business from a stranger. Once a two-hundred-pound man taunted Zulu in spite of our warning. The man kept teasing our pet, until, quick as lightning, Zulu jumped to his shoulder, nipped his ear, and jumped back to safety before the man knew what had happened. Zulu put a stop to his foolishness —but quick!

True, Zulu is getting cross and irritable with

30

people in his old age, but formerly he would enjoy being played with for hours by anyone. He is extremely affectionate, often running from another room to me, just to kiss my hand. And he will sit for hours on Athos's lap while he is painting, to get an occasional stroking. When Athos had influenza, for a week Zulu was so sympathetic that he refused to leave Athos's bedside except for bodily needs. It was one of the most touching scenes of loyalty I have seen manifested by an animal to his master.

Not long ago I saw a rare sight: the sparrow went to nestle close by Zulu under the blanket, keeping him company for an hour.

One of the things about Zulu that seems odd to many people is that he utters a variety of sounds, all of them birdlike. Athos and I know so exactly what each means that he might actually be talking our language. At this moment he is emitting regularly the birdlike chirp that I know means he is contented. And Zulu knows much of what we say to him. For the fun of it, I said to him a moment ago, using the special voice he knows is for him exclusively, "Sing your little song!" In answer, he changed his tune to the little song he knew I expected and would please me. Again I repeat: creatures who understand and love each other know how to express themselves intelligibly to each other.

I have just asked Athos if he wants a Coca-Cola, and he said that he did. And then I said, "Zulu, do you want some Coca-Cola?" He answered that he did!

We never know what is going to happen next in nature nor what effect it will have on us, or on other people either. Take, for example, that starling we had.

I had never seen a bird filled with more nervous energy. He got into all sorts of mischief. He flew about the apartment full of the joy of living, or strutted on the floor, unaware that he was clothed in dull black, and lacked the metallic luster or the dots on the pointed feathers of the mature starling. In his excessive happiness he tried to whistle beautifully, but only guttural, croaking noises came out of his syrinx.

He was entirely too smart. Quickly he learned that whenever I went to the kitchen food was set out. Soon he followed me in and tweaked my ear. I chased him away. But his feelings were not hurt and he returned persistently to peck my ear until, out of desperation, I gave him a morsel. Of course the spoiled bird knew how to manage me thereafter.

I had not known that a bird could have a strong body odor until the starling perched on my shoulder. Then I was aware of his distinct smell, although it was not a particularly offensive one. Ever since, one of the things I want to find out about a bird close at hand is whether or not it has a body odor that I can detect.

The starling liked to get on the dirt of the potted plants and scatter it far and wide, much to my annoyance, as I had to clean up the mess several times a day. He was, of course, searching for insects and worms. He poked his closed bill into the dirt, and then, underground, opened the mandibles—very effective plowing.

He ignored the baby towhee, but liked to romp over the apartment with the blue jay, for both were equal to playing roughly. There was such a brotherly bond between the two that, when the jay sickened and died, for a whole day the starling moped over the loss of his companion.

Starlings, in flocks of thousands, spreading over the country have become destructive and obnoxiously noisy; even our single bird became much of a problem for an apartment. When I compared him with the docile towhee, who appeared mentally deficient in proximity with the starling, I could understand the dither of the concerned ornithologists, who have been wondering what to do about the ever-increasing starlings.

31

As an artist, Athos delights in painting adult starlings. Both of us were amazed by the intelligence of our young bird, and thought him fascinating to have around. When the time came to release him as an adult, we did so, knowing that there would be a definite vacancy in our apartment without him. That was six years ago, and there is no way of computing exactly how many starlings have been fathered by our pet. I wonder how he and his offspring are getting along in the battle of ornithologists versus starlings!

If, in 1890-91, people had left starlings in Europe where they belonged and where there were natural enemies to keep them from becoming too numerous, we would have no problem today in America from this introduced species. Tampering with the balance of nature is the fault of man; it is no fault of the starlings, who should never have been transferred forcibly to a continent that would be ideal for their multiplication.

Among our many birds there was a pair of baby owls that we kept caged. We intended to keep them only as long as they might serve as models for a picture, since they have a reputation for being untamable, and in any event our apartment was not suitable for the raising of great horned owls. Even at a tender age, the birds stood about twenty-two inches high. They ate enormous quantities of food, dozed much of the time, and, waking, flapped their wings for exercise. They behaved admirably, and presented us with no problems whatsoever in the apartment.

The most significant event we remember in connection with them occurred when we tried to release them. Together with the friend who had secured the twins for us from a farmer we rode far from the city with the cage, until we found a locality in which we considered they would be safe from harm.

After Athos placed them on the ground they looked at us pitifully with their huge yellow eyes. They raised their conspicuous ear tufts in alarm. They clapped their bills. They never took their eyes off us as they stood where Athos had placed them, and, in their immaturity, I may say they looked simple and stupid.

Gently we shooed them, trying to impress them with the fact that they were free; this only added to their confusion, and they walked distractedly before us. Athos tried holding them up in the air, but, when he jerked his hand from under them, they merely landed clumsily on the ground.

Finally the realization came to us that the large birds were such babies that they did not know how to fly! We had been deluded by their bigness, whereas they were young birds, not physically strong enough for flight nor capable of taking care of themselves. They appeared simple and stupid, for they were still too young to have self-confidence and the other attributes that come with age. Knowing this, we could not leave them in the country on the ground to starve or be killed in some other manner. There was nothing to do except gather them into the cage and put them in the automobile again.

What to do with the poor things? Taking them back to our few rooms would not solve the question, no matter how much we pitied them, for there we could not give them the right environment in which to develop. We were duty-bound to find a proper home for them.

We were faced with a real problem: no one wanted them, not even the city zoo. We were stymied—almost! To make a long, somewhat rambling story short, we finally found an ornithologist who took them to a boys' camp where birdlore was taught. The birds lived there until the following year, when they were released.

Of course now we no longer live in an apartment and word has gotten around that when someone is perplexed by a bird problem, all he has to do is "call the Menabonis."

This past summer a telephone summons caused me to drive ten miles to get a baby great

Purple Gallinule

horned owl. A couple had rescued him from some dogs, since he was helpless on the ground because one of his wings had been neatly clipped. They did not know, and we can only surmise, that someone had got him as a nestling, kept him until his wing primaries were grown, and then, to keep him from flying away, had knowingly and carefully clipped the primaries on one wing. Whoever it was must have tired of the bird that would not respond as a pet; perhaps getting meat for him during rationing was too much trouble; so he took him to the woods to shift for himself. Had the couple not chanced to find him, there is no question but that he would have died.

I brought him home to Athos. Those huge yellow eyes looked at us questioningly, recalling the two pairs that had looked at us years ago. We did not particularly want a great horned owl, and we could have lived just as happily without this new responsibility. But other eyes were watching us also—the eyes of St. Francis in his shrine. Of course we could not put an end to the owl's life. We would keep him as best we could. The stubby primary quills could have been plucked, so that new ones would grow out quickly, but we could not bring ourselves to inflict pain on the owl— not with the patron saint of the birds watching us. There was no alternative except to decide to place the owl in a cage, keep him until next year, when he will molt his cut primaries and get new feathers naturally. At that time we shall release the adult bird in the country somewhere.

Last night I heard him hoot, asking several times "Who?"

Who, who, indeed, cares for a great horned owl? I have a vague feeling that I am not getting as much from my association with the largest owl in my region as I should. For a long time this morning I stood before the cage and looked at those glassy eyes, fringed with beautiful lashes, watched the conspicuously long ear tufts raise and lower, heard the castanet-clapping of the bill—certainly an inscrutable bird. It disturbs

me to know that as yet I feel no real affection for this creature of nature.

It does not matter to me that others term him the "tiger of the air," fierce and cruel, and that he eats chickens and domestic ducks and is therefore harmful to the agriculturist; if these things make up his character and are entirely natural to the nocturnal bird, well and good. Let the farmer and the owl fight it out in a battle of wits, but let it be a fair, natural fight.

This morning I felt that his eyes were trying to tell me something, but I was not quite ready to know what it was. Could it be that he was saying, "Who are you and other humans to condemn me in any way? Who are you to call me cruel and fierce when you, too, kill poultry to eat? Who are you—God Almighty—to set yourself up as a judge of anything pertaining to my nature? Who—?"

I came away humbled. Perhaps this is the great lesson I am to learn from this bird.

In those apartment days we had birds everywhere, birds walking around, flying from room to room, in cages, some sitting on eggs in a basket nest Athos fastened to the chandelier.

Then there were the birds Athos was painting. My husband's complaint was against nature for not making any day long enough for him to say all he wanted to about his birds. Mine was that I had no means of expressing how I, too, felt about birds. But all this was changed in one exciting day.

The telephone rang one morning and Athos answered it. I heard him say, "How do you do? Yes—certainly—I'll be glad to do it—thank you for asking me. Good-bye."

Filled with curiosity, I asked who it was.

"The editor of the Atlanta *Journal Magazine*," Athos replied. "He wanted to know if I would write an article on birds for him, and I told him that I would."

"Athos!" I cried, horrified at what he had got

into. "You know about birds, you know how to write beautiful Italian, but you do not know how to write in English!"

"Oh, you'll do it," he informed me. "You have always written for your own amusement, now's your chance to write for publication."

"But you said that you would do it!"

"Does it matter whether I sign the article or you sign it? The point is that the editor thinks his readers would like to know more about birds. Don't worry, I'll help you with your article, as you help me in various ways concerning my pictures. Remember that we do everything together."

"When is it supposed to be finished?" I asked.

"He wants it delivered Tuesday morning."

And this was four o'clock on Sunday afternoon! I could waste no time, so I got out my typewriter and faced my problem squarely. I sat there staring at blank paper. How often I had seen Athos looking at a blank canvas. But he always knew what he wanted to record in paint. But what would I say? What did I have to offer?

The day before, I had opened the door to admit the Negro whom I had engaged to wash the windows. I asked him if he had brought any rags. He burst into laughter, then said, "All I's got is rags—and they're on my back!"

I examined myself: "All I's got is thoughts —and they're inside me." How to get them out into words, as Athos expressed himself in paint?

Birds are fun—there was my subject! I must tell how I thought birds were fun, and I must start immediately stringing words together to make an article. Type one word, then the second! That was the way Athos developed a bird picture, simply putting one brush stroke upon the canvas, followed by another and another.

Unfortunately I had had no training in writing, as he had had long training in how to paint. I should have to write as I felt, and let the participles fall where they might. Just let the birds and nature take charge of me!

Tuesday morning, during one of the worst snowfalls Atlanta had had in years, and when transportation was almost at a halt, I went to town to deliver the article. Nothing was said about its having been written by me instead of

Athos, so everything was all right on that score. But they laughed at my having all but broken my neck to get the article to them on Tuesday morning, saying, "Why, you didn't have to come out in this weather. We don't intend to use the article for three weeks!"

Had I known that I had three weeks to prepare my first published work, perhaps it would never have been written, for fear set in. Had I split infinitives, used southern colloquialisms, misspelled words? There was no style, no literary value whatsoever, no anything that I could remember, for I had not made a carbon copy. In fact, I could remember hardly anything about it except that I had ended the article: "Birds are grand, people are grander!"

It was foolish of me to have been afraid, for the day the article appeared in print people telephoned all day, and during the following week the postman brought stacks of letters from friends and utter strangers. There were no references to the literary aspects of the article, for people were occupied only with expressing to us how much pleasure they got from birds, and they were pleased to have kindred souls on whom they could unload their emotions. All of us had found a way of overcoming gnawing repression, and of opening our hearts.

Our birds sang. They did not bother with singing *technique*. They just opened up and sang fully, according to their individual natures! If their songs fell on receptive ears, well and good. . . . I think that I have never pitied anyone so much as the man who told me that he hated the mockingbirds that woke him early in the mornings, and that to put a stop to their dad-blasted noise, he shot mockingbirds at every opportunity. No writing skill of mine or of anyone else would ever make him open his heart to birds.

Shortly, a friend asked me to be the guest speaker at her club and I accepted, glad to have another way of giving to others what I possessed —my birds. I had no training for public speak-

ing, but—I thought—if I could take a first step at writing my thoughts, then I could take a first step at expressing myself vocally.

In the room full of women, my friend arose to introduce me. She was so frightened that her knees could hardly hold her up and her hands and voice were visibly trembling. I was supposed to make my audience enjoy my birds, but I was as scared as my friend. Fear was a bull charging toward me. The first thing I had to do was to grab the bull by the horns and throw it. I would swing that bull by the tail! If I could somehow get out the first sentence, then the rest would be easy.

I spoke my first sentence, but before I had a chance to say the next one, a woman popped up to tell her favorite bird story! She could not formally wait until the end of my talk to express herself—and neither could others. Never since have I had such a talkative audience. But that day, although I stood on my feet for an hour, I spoke no longer than ten or fifteen minutes and we had a joyful time together, swapping experiences and birdlore.

Fine! I had written a bird article and given a talk, and that was that. Or so I thought at the moment. Just as when Athos painted his first bird picture he had thought that would be the end of it and it turned out that it was only the beginning, so it was with my expressing my feelings about birds. I did not deliberately decide to write and talk about birds the rest of my life, but somehow the forces of nature swept me into these activities. The odd thing about the whole affair is that as soon as we've finished with one subject, another has come up, demanding that we tackle it next. At this very moment I see Athos beginning a new picture—why, he began one yesterday —and the day before he had drawn still another bird! There are three pictures being painted at once. It is no wonder he complains that no day is long enough. As for me, in my living room this minute is a bird story progressing to a climax, outside my window is a new pet that I'm anxious

American Robin

ROBIN AND BUCKEYE
ICHAUWAY PLANTATION

to write about, and up in a pine is a wild bird calling to me to give him space in a book.

If we have given our birds to people, it is a small contribution compared to the marvelous ways in which people have enriched our lives. We shall never be able to express our gratitude. I find myself angry at the conventions of society that prevent spontaneous expression of affection between human beings. I don't see a single example in nature of the creatures not expressing themselves unreservedly in any way they please, and the irony of it is that they are called "dumb creatures," "without souls!"

Thank God, I can now go to the living room and tell Charlotte (a bird) exactly how much I love her, and she will tell me how much she loves me. If that won't be fun, then I don't know what fun is.

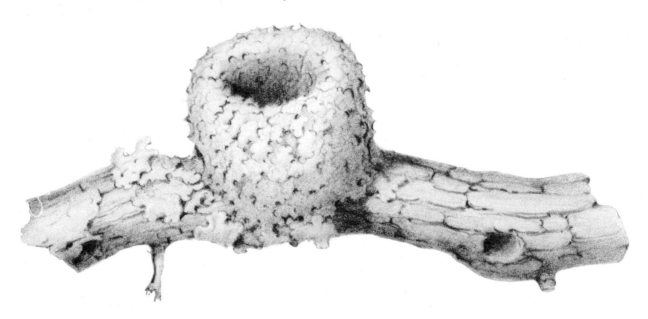

CHAPTER THREE

ATHOS IS OUTDOORS TODAY, probably supervising the dam building. Birds come to us all the time—even the rock mason's name is Byrd! He is a good Negro worker, and the dam will soon be finished. We are anxious to have the lake for our ducks.

I pause a moment, remembering our apartment-living days. I believe this is the right time to tell of our bathtub babies, but before I give their history I should give an account of their mallard duck parents.

The Duke and Duchess arrived in high style, in a palanquin borne upon the shoulder of an expressman. They were "to the manor born," and, in our apartment, we hurriedly prepared the best accommodations we could at the moment, making an enclosure on top of our dining-room table and strewing it with pine needles. We hoped they would not squawk about it, for it was a far cry from the grandeur of "Blue Springs Farm."

A more regal, properly mannered pair we had never seen. They exhibited no wildness, although the fact that they did not make a sound while they visited us showed a trace of wild heritage. They demonstrated uneasiness only when they were taken one at a time to the filled bathtub several times a day to swim. They did not like to be separated for even the time it took to go from one room to another.

While Athos painted their portrait, they posed beautifully.

We were amused one morning to find a newly laid egg on top of our dining-room table! Eggs probably never appeared in stranger circumstances. As this occurred every day, we took it to mean that the Duke and the Duchess were contented while visiting us.

The day came when we reluctantly bade farewell to the pair, who went to live at another manor. But we considered that the eggs rightly belonged to us, as a token of the Duke and Duchess's appreciation of our hospitality.

How could we hatch the eggs?

As usual, a friend offered to settle the problem. At her place the eggs were put under a setting hen. The hen was clumsy and promptly broke some of the eggs. After the lapse of some time, early one morning our friend telephoned to say excitedly, "The first duckling has hatched, but the hen stepped on it, killing it. Come get the eggs before something happens to the rest of them!"

Here was another dilemma. How could we keep the eggs warm during the transportation and the rest of the hatching period? Luckily we thought of a solution. We'd take our electric heating pad with us!

At our friend's house we plugged in the electric pad, and, when it was warm, we placed it over the eggs in the basket. On the way home in the automobile the eggs knew no difference between the pad's warmth and that of the hen.

And so, with the electric heat of a hot pad, the hatching was completed in our bathroom. Had the four ducklings been out of doors, instead of in a white-tiled bathroom, they would have been downy examples of camouflage. They were yellowish and brownish in color, which would have made them nearly invisible among the vegetation. They cocked their little heads to look at us alertly with beady black eyes and from their broad bills came peep-peeps, demanding attention. They nibbled at our hands with their rubbery bills, giving the sensation of vibration. We cuddled them and they liked it. My soul! They thought we were their mama and papa!

They "took to water like ducks," needing no swimming or diving lessons. They stood up in the water and shook their little stubs of wings. Then they began playing tag and follow-the-leader. How their webbed feet could paddle!

We gave them lettuce in the water, and they ate out of our hands. They would peck at anything, and if nothing was handy, they continued to use their bills, blowing bubbles in the water. And what a noise those four little bills could make. In their cage drinking cup they made the same clatter. They took mouthfuls of sand to the water cup, and made a messy place out of their wire-bottomed cage. They ate constantly when not swimming or dozing.

We watched their prodigious growth every day, marveling as the encased quills began to poke through their down. As babies they were so cunning that I did not wish them to grow up too fast, even to be as handsomely arrayed as the Duke and the Duchess.

We soon discovered that an apartment was no place to raise ducks. For that matter, any birds were out of place there and, carrying the thought further, we knew we, too, were out of place in city quarters, with our increasing interest in birds and our joy in having them live with us. It follows naturally that we found a house to rent that had a generous acreage. And so we gleefully took our next major step toward a better way of living.

One of our objectives had been to find land that had a brook, for we did not want our ducklings always to be bathtub babies. We had in mind to make a small dam in the brook, thereby raising the water level a foot or so to form a pool for them where they would be penned in.

However, after moving from the apartment to the rented country home, we found we were too busy getting settled the first few days to begin the building of a dam.

A few days later, after a rainstorm, we went to see how the shower had affected the stream. To our surprise and disappointment, the rain had caused the brook to swell into a muddy torrent,

almost out of its banks. We had to abandon our plans, or else we should have found dam, pen, and ducklings washed away someday by the turbulent water.

With a feeling of sorrow and frustration, we built a pen on the hill close to the house, without adequate swimming facilities for our ducklings. We told a friend about it, and he offered to help the situation. He said to dig a hole in the pen, run water pipes to it, and he would bring us an old bathtub to put in the ground.

Those ducklings were destined to be bathtub babies. Never having known anything different, they joyfully jumped into their brimming tub and had great fun diving in deeper water than they had had formerly. After all, it is not every duck that can have a slick white-enamel bathtub!

All this was years ago, and those mallards—one drake and three ducks—were destined to make still another move, farther into the country. Their first springtime here they got busy with nest building on the hills and that season produced fifty-seven babies!

Now, at last, the ducks are getting their lake. While the dam is being constructed, they often fly down to see how it is getting along. I, too, learned how to fly when I left the city to live in the country, and right now I myself shall fly down to see the dam.

A few moments ago Ike, our Negro who has worked for us certain days a week for six years, said to me, "I was jus' tellin' them that they jus' ought to come to see our place." Then he paused, realizing that he had said "our place," and continued, "I calls it ours, but it ain't really mine."

"Oh, yes, it is yours, too! You keep right on calling it 'ours.' "

He accepted what I had said, and went on talking about the dam for the lake, which is his project almost entirely; he was the one who had insisted that it be started without any more delay and had engaged the various workers. We

40

Mallard

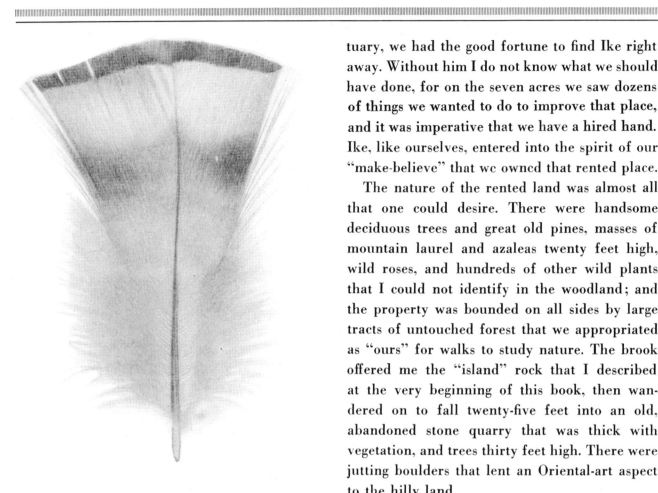

tuary, we had the good fortune to find Ike right away. Without him I do not know what we should have done, for on the seven acres we saw dozens of things we wanted to do to improve that place, and it was imperative that we have a hired hand. Ike, like ourselves, entered into the spirit of our "make-believe" that we owned that rented place.

The nature of the rented land was almost all that one could desire. There were handsome deciduous trees and great old pines, masses of mountain laurel and azaleas twenty feet high, wild roses, and hundreds of other wild plants that I could not identify in the woodland; and the property was bounded on all sides by large tracts of untouched forest that we appropriated as "ours" for walks to study nature. The brook offered me the "island" rock that I described at the very beginning of this book, then wandered on to fall twenty-five feet into an old, abandoned stone quarry that was thick with vegetation, and trees thirty feet high. There were jutting boulders that lent an Oriental-art aspect to the hilly land.

I say that it was almost perfect, but it lacked a fence to protect us against dogs. There were other nuisances. When we were in the deep woods standing breathless and still to hear some pileated woodpeckers as they approached us, riders came galloping through; and when, at our new feeding station, we were watching a brown-headed nuthatch that we were trying to learn to spot-identify, the neighbor children came galloping through on their broom-stick "horses." There were many more instances like those that made us determine that if at some future time we really owned land one of the most important things we would have to do to make it a true bird sanctuary would be to fence it in.

Nevertheless, we enjoyed our country place thoroughly. There was the screened porch in which we could keep the housebirds; we had built two large aviaries for our outdoor birds in captivity. Had the place been fenced in, we

have let him spend his time with it, although there were other problems in the upkeep of a sanctuary that he should have attended to. Ike has worked like a slave to make the lake a reality, for the pure love of making a dream come true.

I ended the conversation with "Ike, the lake is your baby—go play with your baby now!"

As he left the house, I heard him singing a Negro spiritual, a very happy man in "our place." Ike loves the birds as much as we do and therefore, without any prompting save from within himself, he will work unstintingly at anything pertaining to them. He is a rare character, in these days when most laborers do as little as they can get away with. He says there are so many things he wants to do here that "the day jus' ain't long enough."

When we moved from the apartment to the rented country place that preceded this sanc-

could have let many of our caged birds have their freedom, but we did take them from the aviaries often for outside exercise while we watched over them.

The wild birds must have passed around the word that we were preparing for them as fine accommodations as we could, for all sorts started coming to us. Even a young squab walked up the driveway one day. Where Blondie came from we never knew, for in the surrounding neighborhood no one had pigeons, and her history remained a mystery. (We remembered how the parakeet came to us in the apartment building. Perhaps St. Francis had guided these two birds straight to us.) Blondie could not yet fly or find her own food; we had to force-feed her until she was old enough to eat alone, and to prepare the right living quarters for her. Naturally we were given a mate for our pigeon. But the really wild birds had a vast area in which to find natural living conditions to their tastes and plentiful food, for the surrounding countryside had many large estates and small farms, and even a large-scale county park.

Had we wished to we could have walked the three blocks' distance to the park, but instead of going swimming in the beautiful artificial pool, we preferred to get under our private waterfall; had we wished to make reservations for one of the outdoor grills, we could have done so, but we liked to have our impromptu picnics with friends at any spot in our woods that we chose on the moment. We could have played golf on the fine eighteen-hole links, yet we chose to follow with our eyes the birds that took us on the rounds and on whom we kept score cards. We never went to a horse show there, liking better our daily bird show all to ourselves; nor did we attend a polo game, liking better a game of hide-and-seek with a red fox that came daily to drink at our waterfall. The park was a wonderful place for city folk, but we had no need of the park's offerings.

We could not have worked harder on the acreage had we had title to the place. The paths had to be cleared of luxuriant poison ivy for the sake of friends who were allergic to it. We left the dead trees standing for the woodpeckers, but fallen trees were cut by Ike for the sake of appearance and to furnish wood for the fireplace. We planted shrubs about the house, and a hedge where it was logical to have one, separating our house from the next one. We lost weight at the physical labor, but felt in exuberant health and happiness.

Perhaps we had been cooped up so long in a city apartment that we were driven by some strong indefinable pressure, because of which we could appreciate an incident that concerned Ike one day. A windstorm had blown down a hollow beech tree, and Athos told me that Ike would be occupied with cutting it for two or three days, even though other pressing duties would have to remain undone. That morning Ike started upon the job, and at noon when Athos went to tell him to come to lunch he found Ike dripping with perspiration. To Athos's amazement, the entire tree had been cut into firewood.

"Ike!" Athos exclaimed incredulously. "Why did you work so hard? You need not have cut the whole tree in these few hours."

"I tell you, boss," Ike explained. "I's got high blood pressure and I simply can't work slow."

We tried to make Ike take it easy after lunch, and set him to work polishing silver, but we soon saw that he was miserable at the sedentary chore and let him escape outdoors, where his heart was, to tackle other hard jobs.

Ike never liked the sunken bathtub for the ducks, and repeatedly said, "Miss, it jus' ain't natchul for our ducks to swim in thata thing." And so—coming back to the present—Ike is now working hard for the lake he is determined to have. His heart is in "our" sanctuary, and he takes great pride in all we have done together;

we voice our appreciation to him, giving him all the credit for many achievements.

He has brought an ancient Negro named Uncle Charlie to work on the dam project, who, like "Uncle Remus," talks to the birds as though they were people. This in itself has been delightful to hear, but not extraordinary, for often I find myself doing the same thing.

However, when I left my desk a few minutes ago to join the company of the two Negroes working at the dam building, and as I stood near Uncle Charlie as he was breaking rocks, I overheard his private conversation with the rocks.

"Now you jus' sit still here a lil minute. This ain't goin' to hurt you much. See?" He hit the rock with his sledge hammer. "Now that warn't bad, wuz it?" The rock slid to one side. "No, don't you try to squirm, you jus' hold still." The rock slid some more. "Come back here an' act good. You can't get away. Behave yo'self! I's tryin' my bestest to go easy an' not hurt you none." He hit the rock again and, as it was finally the right size, he laid it aside with a pat of the hand. "See, I done tol' you I wuzn't goin' to hurt you much. It's all over now an' you jus'

set there an' rest a spell now. You ain't goin' to be bothered no mo'."

As I walked away I heard Ike jubilantly singing: "When I gets to Heaven, goin' put on my shoes, goin' to walk all over God's Heaven—"

I, too, feel like shouting all over my little heaven-on-earth, in gratitude that I have such goodly folk as these with me.

I left Athos at the dam, and I wouldn't be at all surprised if he does not come into the studio all day. It is his "day off," from painting, and he works alongside his helpers. "Works?" I should say that it is his day for "play." He is selecting the prettiest rocks to be used on the face of the dam, where we can always see them. The lake is for the ducks, but I often wonder if it is not in reality a monument to dreams.

This morning as I idly looked up at the blue sky I saw a broad-winged hawk circling. With scarcely a wingbeat, he sailed with the wind until he was almost out of sight, and then obligingly turned around to retrace his course for my benefit. He continued to soar directly overhead for fully fifteen minutes, and my mind soared with him.

Carolina Chickadee

I heard the pecking of a woodpecker close by, but I did not bother to search him out. Soon he came into my vision—a downy; and later I saw a red-bellied woodpecker. There was no effort on my part, the birds were coming to me.

Three, four, five times some songbirds flashed by me, and I did not trouble to turn my head or leave my bench to search them out, so as to be able to say that I had seen five such-and-such species. I was happy in my ignorance of what they were and they, no doubt, were happy in not being stalked.

I heard the "dee-dee-dee" of a Carolina black-capped chickadee, but I did not see him. It wasn't a matter of importance to me to see a chickadee for the *n*th time; it did matter to me that he was near by, giving his call that brought with it pleasant recollections.

A white-breasted nuthatch walked up a tree trunk and then, head down, descended, all the while poking into the crevices of the bark to get his lunch.

I heard a pileated woodpecker not far away. Many times in the past I would have gone stealthily in search of a glimpse of him, but not today; I was content just to know that he liked to live in our sanctuary.

As I lay motionless, I saw bluebirds and wood thrushes come to the dogwood near me to eat the berries undisturbed. These were migrating birds that find in this sanctuary hundreds of the trees to whose fruit they are partial.

No, there was nothing unusual about my bird watching today, and yet it was perfect enjoyment. Why?

There was a time that I was all in a lather over my ignorance of the birds. Athos had already had exhibitions of his pictures at many places over the nation, and the indications were that he would continue painting birds. It behooved me as well as Athos to know all about birds. He had studied them since early childhood in Italy, had continued to study them after coming

to the United States, and knew a great deal about the Georgia bird life. I, who had lived continually among Georgia birds, could count on my fingers the ones I could identify.

Through our experiences with birds in the apartment, I had reached a fever pitch of desire to know more about them and of the events that I sensed were changing the course of my life. But at the time we moved to the country, I did not know there was any kind of hawk save the "chicken hawk"; I did not know the difference between a wood thrush and the brown thrasher, the state bird of Georgia; I was unaware of the differences between a summer tanager and a scarlet tanager; I knew no woodpeckers save the red-headed, nor any sparrows except the English sparrow. I did not know any warblers existed! I knew that the "bald-headed" eagle was the national emblem bird, and that there were some sea gulls on the coast. But daily my colossal ignorance was showing, and I had a tremendous job ahead of me to learn all I wanted to about the birds.

Athos had a headstart on me, and, try as I might, I knew I could never catch up with him, for while I was learning the common birds, he was learning the rarer ones. He had the edge on me with his memory for color, perception of detail, family characteristics, species, flight patterns, and songs. He had had such a thorough knowledge of European birds that the birds of America were not difficult for him to learn. Always I should lag a mile behind him.

I pored over the bird books, cramming up on them as if I were studying for school examinations. But let me get outdoors with, say, warblers, and, to save my life, I could not identify any except the hooded, yellow-throated, and myrtle. Quickly I learned the fox sparrow, but the other sparrows were so many little brownish birds that looked exactly alike to my undiscerning eye. How could I ever learn to differentiate between a downy and a hairy woodpecker? I was in a dither, and studied the books harder.

Some days outdoors we would see only blue jays, crows, cardinals, or bluebirds, which I knew well, and other days there would be vireos, thrushes, wrens, swallows, grosbeaks; and I found that all those birds must be named positively as: red-eyed vireo, hermit thrush, Carolina wren, tree swallow, or rose-breasted grosbeak—individuals—not to be classed in a mere general way.

I had written two bird articles for the newspaper, and I had to know my facts about birds in order to write more; already I was giving bird talks to organizations, and no matter how prepared I was for my set speech, afterwards all manner of unexpected questions would be asked of me. It had even been suggested that Athos paint the pictures for a book and that I write the text! In many ways, I realized that I had to know birds thoroughly, and I worked hard at my new interest.

Fortunately I had a good teacher who was not impatient with my ignorance. Athos told me to make mental notes first of the size and striking marks, and then of details, such as the color of the lores, outer primary feather construction, under-tail coverts and mandibles. His trained eyes took in all those things at a glance. But they were difficult for me, for I had not yet learned the topography of a bird. And so I set about learning what was considered the chin, throat, breast, belly, sides, and flanks; and what all the other segmented parts of birds were called, and which make up exact descriptions of them when filled in with colors and markings.

There were all sorts of other things to learn. For instance, I had to find out about the feet, tail feathers, bill, and tongue of a woodpecker, and learn too that those same anatomic details in the ruby-throated hummingbird were dissimilar; and that the feet, tail, bill, and tongue of a woodcock were still different, and so on, and on, and on. Athos was not disturbed by my

dilemma; he was serenely adding up his facts little by little until they made wholes.

One day I was so dejected that I exclaimed, "I shall never learn all about the birds, no matter how hard I try!"

"You try too hard," Athos counseled. "Take it easy—relax. Go outdoors to enjoy yourself, and if an unknown bird happens along, study him intently, and when you return to the house, look him up in a bird book. The next time you see him outdoors, you will know him. That's all there is to it, and gradually your list of well-known birds will grow.

"But, Sara, it is really not so important to know all the birds by proper names, if that lack is going to spoil your pleasure in watching them. What does it matter if you don't know a Henslow's sparrow or magnolia warbler this very minute? Just enjoy your fox sparrow and your hooded warbler, leaving the unknown birds to learn in due course of time. There is no possibility of learning ornithology in six easy lessons. It takes continued interest and time. And no one knows it all!"

And so I learned to take it easy, to relax, and in due course of time to learn my nature lessons—and above all not to fret over the fact that I should never know all about ornithology. But gradually, little by little, I have been adding up my facts. Today didn't I know instantly that the hawk so high in the sky was a broad-winged? The woodpeckers were downy and red-bellied, and so on? Had I ruined my resting period by chasing arduously after the five songbirds that flashed by I daresay that I could have identified them positively. But it was too perfect a day to work hard; I was simply enjoying myself.

No, I do not have to worry any longer about knowing every bird this very minute. I have come to the realization that if I knew all there would no longer be the zest of anticipation.

Yesterday afternoon late, after Ike had finished the dam building, and while I was driving him to the streetcar line, he said to me, "Miss, I wants to get dressed in my Sunday clothes someday an' come out to have my picture took standin' by the dam when the water is coming over it. I wants to have my Bible in my han', opened at a certain chapter 'bout Lazarus. Yessum, from the bottom to the top, from the beginnin' to the end."

This last sentence was obscure to me, but I gathered that he was referring to something Biblical that tied in with his building and finishing of the dam.

"An', miss, I wants Emma lying at my feets."

"Emma?" I asked, not knowing what he was talking about.

"Yessum, Emma. In the Bible the dog licked the wounds of Lazarus."

"Oh, yes, Emma," I echoed. I had not noticed before that all these years Ike has been thinking that our dog's name was "Emma" instead of Yama. (It tickled me no less, since for years I had called Ike's son Harrison by the sound of the name as he pronounced it, "Hasson.") I did not correct Ike's calling our dog "Emma."

"Please, ma'am, can I have my picture took like that with Emma?"

"Of course! When the lake is filled and there is a waterfall, you can have your picture took exactly as you want it, Ike."

Since that conversation I have wondered what Ike meant by wanting his photograph taken with Yama in that manner. "The dog licked the wounds of Lazarus." Can it be a symbol to Ike? I had not previously known that the dog meant so much to him. Yet, does not Yama lick Ike's face in warm greeting every time they meet, as though Ike were his long-lost friend returned at last? Does not Yama love Ike, as he loves everyone, with a great passion, whether he be white or black, young or old?

After being with Yama for four years, I have yet to see him demonstrate any ugly traits of character; he is beautiful in body, beautiful in spirit. He has won no beauty contests, for he has never been entered in a dog show, nor has he won any field-trial ribbons, because he was not trained for hunting. But this Irish setter is getting his just dues in a book now, which is a human vanity on my part. He definitely has a role in all that goes on in our place.

Yama loves the birds.

Right now, as I look out my window, I see him stretched out asleep in the sunshine, and on top of him is the silver Sebright bantam rooster—yes, squatting on Yama as though it were the most logical place for a rooster to be. I am always amused to see the rooster raise himself to full importance on top of Yama, crow for all he is worth, and yet not even awaken Yama! In truth, it *is* logical for this particular rooster to be atop Yama, for the dog helped raise the orphan, as he has helped raise many another creature.

Shortly after we moved to the country, a friend —named Friend—gave the Irish setter puppy to us. I wondered if Yama, with a fine pedigree from famous hunting ancestors, would be on good terms with our birds or if he would hunt them down. Athos had no misgivings about it, for he knew that he could train Yama to be what we wanted him to be, a suitable companion in all that we did.

Right away Yama was subjected to birds, the first ones being the mallard ducklings. The puppy did not have to be taught to be gentle and considerate of the downy little things. He sensed that he must be careful with his playmates, whereas with Athos he could play rough-and-tumble. I could not understand how Yama knew the difference. The ducklings had no fear of Yama; they knew that he was there for them to scramble all over, nibble at, and explore. They liked to play around his loose lips; Yama would obligingly open his mouth, and, with their bodies almost entirely between his jaws, they would peck around inside. This became a favorite pastime. Outdoors, when Yama ran with his duck-

Bobwhite

lings waddling under him, he worked his legs carefully in order not to step on them. As they grew older, one mallard drake took delight in running with his head poked inside Yama's mouth—a neat trick indeed—and a sport that the two have indulged in daily for years!

Along with his love for his birds Yama developed a keen responsibility toward protecting them from any harm. Let him hear a bird alarm-call, and he jumps up, all attention, looking frantically about for the cause of the disturbance. (Again I repeat, birds and animals talk to each other.)

Not long ago we were in the house, Yama watching his new squirrel babies, when, from the valley, came the squawking of the ducks in distress. Yama flew out the unlatched screened door, Athos dashed out, and I trailed along. We were just in time to see a Cooper's hawk swoop down to make a strike at a duck! The hawk was within a foot of the duck and then—the streak of red lightning flashed upon his vision! The hawk made a quick change in plans and high-tailed it to safety. Yama chased after the hawk, and did not return to us until he was satisfied that the hawk had left our sanctuary. Entirely on his own initiative, Yama had saved the life of his duck.

Yama has a fine sense of discrimination. He knows who is an enemy and who is a pet of his masters. We have had innumerable tame hawks with whom he has been on friendly terms from the moment they entered our lives. The hawks have no cause to fear Yama, and accept him soon as harmless. However, they do not have the sense of humor that he does, and find nothing funny in the way he teases them to try to get them into a playful mood: they tolerate his nonsense, and he, in turn, respects their not wishing to become too intimate.

There is nothing that Yama likes better than a box of baby birds on the floor that he can watch for hours on end. He cannot bear to leave his babies, even to eat his one meal a day. His big nose nudges them ever so gently, and then he starts kissing them, that is, licking them. The young birds do not object, but his kisses make the birds wet and then they get cold, so that we must forbid his showering them with kisses. Although he knows that he will be scolded again, he gradually sneaks up to his babies, and, after an hour of patient waiting, licks them again, in the hope that we are not looking. He simply cannot help it, he must kiss them! If we put the box somewhere higher than he can reach, as punishment, he cries so pitifully that we have to give the babies back to him, with the firm admonition "No kissing!"

Let the babies run about on the floor, and Yama is in ecstasy. He lets his great body down to a lying position—in slow motion, for fear of crushing one of his beloveds. They nestle close to their nurse for warmth, getting under his neck or his legs, and he will keep a rigid position in order not to disturb or hurt them. If he can steal a kiss, he thinks he is very smart to outwit us.

I remember the time we had the quicksilver baby bobwhites. Yama was in a frenzy because they darted about so fast that he could not keep up with them. He learned about quail from them, and yesterday when we were walking in our woods and a covey flew up in front of him, he stopped dead still to watch them with interest. (Did he know that they were his very own babies, now grown and free?) He knows nothing of hunting quail with guns; he does know what it is to love them.

His one fault, if it can be called a fault, for he does not know anything about mudstains on clothes, is that he jumps with unrestrained joy all over visitors when they arrive. We cannot expect him to hold his genial nature in check and have company manners, since not a single person has co-operated with us in the attempt to train him. No one has the heart to step hard on his feet, and whipping him is unthinkable when he loves people so ardently. If we chain him, his feelings are so hurt and he looks so pitiful that our guests make us untie him.

After we have calmed him down from his wholehearted greeting of the visitors, it is Yama who starts showing off his birds. When the Canada geese won't make a display of themselves, but show annoyance at being disturbed, Yama knows that he can get the proper response from the wild turkeys, who are show-offs. Then Yama runs up the hill to the aviary, suggesting that everybody come on to see what is waiting there. He wants them to hurry-hurry to the valley to see his ducks in their puddle (which will soon be a lake), and gets right in the puddle too. And, oh, if the visitors want to take a long bird-walk, the more miles the better, Yama is in the seventh heaven. He can show our friends lots of wild birds, if only they will go look for them with him.

A dog's life with naturalists is all that Yama seems to desire. Now he is in the house, and a few minutes ago he went to the glass door to look out with us to see a pileated woodpecker we had heard close by, and who was hanging upside down on a branch of dogwood eating the berries. Yama misses nothing that goes on in the sanctuary.

He does not appreciate art, but he likes to be in the studio while Athos paints, for any time he craves attention he can go to Athos, who will continue to paint with one hand and pat Yama's head with the other. He does not appreciate writing either, but he likes me to be at my typewriter, as I am at this moment, so that he can come to kiss my ears! He would rather have affection than eat.

He wishes that I would come with him for a walk this very minute—and I shall humor him!

Wild Turkey

CHAPTER FOUR

*A*s I BREAKFASTED this Thanksgiving morning, I saw one of the sights I like best, our tame wild turkeys leaping in the air out of sheer joy. They ran a couple of feet with wings open, sprang into the air two or three feet, landed, ran again, sprang, repeating their antics over and over, for no reason at all except that they were glad to be alive on a beautiful morning.

Now that I have come to my desk, from my window I see that two gobblers are playing a game that is very silly: facing in the same direction, they walk briskly around and around a pine, until I should think they would get dizzy. As though at a prearranged signal, they stop suddenly at the same time, turn in the opposite direction to go again around and around the pine. Then stop—turn—go round and round, playing this ring-around-the-rosy for half an hour or more, utterly happy. Finally one will think that to frisk with Yama, with whom they grew up, will be more fun.

Since the wild turkey, of stock unmixed with domestic fowl, is becoming very rare, Athos was at a loss some years ago as to where and how to secure a pair of living birds. Thanks to having many friends, it proved not to be a problem long, for soon after we moved to the country, a pair of turkeys came to us.

All my life I had looked unseeingly at domestic turkeys, but when this pair arrived, for the first time I actually *saw* turkeys. Upon seeing them in bright sunlight, what impressed me most was the feather coloration; their luster was of new copper, burnished bronze, and red-hot iron, yet in certain lights, as the birds moved about

their pen, there were greenish-purple glitters. I should have been most impressed by the chestnut tail tips and upper-tail coverts, distinguishing these eastern wild turkeys from the domestic species, who have white at those places; or I should have noted that the primary feather white and black bars differed somewhat from those of the barnyard fowl, but such things did not cause me to marvel as the metallic colors did.

However, I began noticing other features, notably that they were smaller and more streamlined than the domestic turkeys I had seen. The "beard" of the gobbler hung like a stiff tassel from the center of the upper chest where the feathers parted. He stuck out his chest, full of hot air. On his pinkish-lavender legs he walked deliberately and with dignity.

There was a certain fascination about the featherless head of the gobbler, as the colors changed on the flat forehead from pale aquamarine to ultramarine and the deepening color on the cheeks shaded into violent bluish-purple. The wrinkled neck and wattle looked as though a child had crudely quilted and stuffed a piece of red leather, getting tired of making small creases and ending the bottom with three uneven lumps. As I watched the strange head, the colors changed from pale blue to white, with only touches of pink on the back of the head and neck, and splotches of red on the lowest white lumps—a magical transition from the first strong colors I had seen. How nice to be able to change colors to go with whatever colorful mood one is in!

The erectile process grew over the nose, and was either drawn in so that it was inconspicuous or it was elongated and dangled limp over the bill looking as if it were in the way. It was either pale pinkish or blood-red. What was the purpose of this bit of flesh? He had a frowning expression caused by the crease in the center of the forehead and the overhanging flesh above the brown eyes.

I thought that the hen had a much prettier

head than the vain male. She had only a small erectile process, and she had little brownish hairlike feathers on her forehead and down the back of her neck, and not so much of the queer wrinkled and wattled ornamentation as the gobbler. Of small build, she was sleek and dainty. The hen seemed to be demure and content that she was less conspicuous than her spouse, although her green-gold and bronze colors were beautiful.

The gobbler was a show-off. When he puffed himself up, each feather standing on end, there was a deep velvety blackness in the shadows that gave him a different aspect. As he strutted around the hen, I had a rear view of his fanned tail, showing the whitish quills of the long upright feathers. Below, looking as though it had been stuck into the body as an afterthought, was the "feather duster." He dragged his stiff wing primaries on the ground, one wing at a time or both of them, disregarding the fact that he was wearing off the feather tips. As he strutted he made a "tsck" noise, then extended his head and gobbled three times. All the while the hen paid slight attention to him, as she contentedly pecked among the leaves, with her trilling, rolling voice coming forth at regular intervals.

They were startlingly striking birds in a pen, but when we brought them from the rented place to our new fenced sanctuary and turned them loose to roam over the acreage, the gobbler took to the woods wildly. For three days we did not catch sight of him in the natural habitat, no matter how much we searched for him with the aid of Yama. Finally he sprang from almost under Athos's feet. Yama and Athos drove him back to the house, many times almost losing sight of him. But Yama by then knew what Athos wanted of him as a dog, and the gobbler rejoined the other turkey to become tame again. A good deal later, when the hen went to the woods to make herself a nest, we searched high and low for her. Not until we had carefully noted the

direction in which she went every day after eating, and without letting her know that we were watching her, did we discover her sitting perfectly still on her nest—right where we had often looked for her and not seen her, because of her protective coloration.

When we first got the turkeys they were wild. Although the hen soon began eating bits of raw meat from Athos's hands, the gobbler never got so intimate. The hen did not object to our watching her take a dust bath; she shook and wallowed in the dry dirt with complete satisfaction and abandon. An odd thing about the turkeys was that during rain or snow they refused to go under shelter. At night they slept on their outdoor perches, and in the daytime preferred the outdoors also.

One fine spring day, where we first had them at the rented place, we discovered that the hen had selected a place under their shelter to make a nest of leaves in hollowed dirt in which to lay her speckled eggs. Nor did the gobbler molest her in any way. We had heard so much of the difficulty of raising turkeys due to rain killing the poults, that Athos took the eggs from the nest one at a time, substituting chicken eggs to fool the hen. We placed the turkey eggs in an electric incubator.

It proved to be a wise course, for the hen got sick. Immediately Athos put her into a pen to herself, and we read all the literature we had about the diseases of gallinaceous birds. In vain we sought a description that fitted the symptoms of her illness; she merely drooped and would not eat. In desperation we sent a specimen of her droppings to an ornithologist friend at the University of Georgia, with an appeal to him to suggest something that we could do for the poor hen, who had not touched food for nine days.

Back came a special-delivery letter, saying that nothing could be found that indicated what could be wrong with her. He said that a great deal is yet to be learned about turkey diseases and their cure. He suggested that drops of ipecac be given to her. If she died (and he was sure that she would die), he asked that the body be sent to the university for study, as he was keen to examine it.

We wrote to him that we were very sorry to disappoint him, but "the hen had recovered." By the time his letter had arrived, the hen, of her own volition, had started to eat. We gave her the ipecac anyway, and perhaps it helped her to recover more quickly.

Shortly thereafter she began laying another clutch of eggs and, because she deserved a reward, we let her keep the eggs. When she had her three youngsters, after twenty-eight days of setting, Athos made an exit for them from their pen, so that she could take them onto the lawn. She never took them far, and brought them back to the pen often for food and water and for the night. We had to shoo them back to shelter when we anticipated rain. Despite her care, however, the hen raised only one of her chicks.

Of the little turkeys hatched in the incubator, four survived in perfect condition under our care. One nice day we took their rearing cage outdoors and set them free on the lawn to peck at the grass and among the leaves. They tried their stubby wings and ran to their hearts' content. When they got separated from each other they uttered loud distress calls; then Athos recalled the poults by whistling a hencall. We were very careful to keep them from getting wet. During the middle of the hot days they rested, completely relaxed except for their alert, keen eyes.

It was amusing to see turkeys a few weeks old strut. They looked like the pine-cone turkeys of Thanksgiving table decorations.

As they grew, they were subjected to much handling and were as tame as could be imagined. I must add, also, that they had a great deal of patience, for they posed for innumerable photographers; once, for movies, they staged a first-class fight among themselves. Strangers always caused them to set up a united clatter, and they would gobble at any unusual noise, although flash bulbs had no effect upon them. They had a strong attachment for their pen, and all would flee to it together, but would not protest much when Athos picked them up to return to a good photographing place on the lawn.

The old gobbler was master of the pen and was respected at all times by the others, when they became adult. But the young gobblers strutted around each other much of the time and had many a fight. One pair that we had raised Athos gave to a friend. In their new environment they reverted to wildness immediately, not apparently recognizing even Athos in their new pen. However, soon our friend tamed them.

The descendants of the original pair are now in our sanctuary enjoying themselves. They like to take walks with us over the acres, but when they come to the brook they are afraid to cross it. Many a time Athos has had to lift them bodily over the water so that they might continue to follow us. The sillies—the brook was no more than a foot or two wide! They do not have clipped wings, yet they have made no attempt to fly over the fence. To gain attention, they strut hour after hour for our visitors. One even likes being held in our arms, so that children's hands may "beat the drum" on his air-filled chest.

Today is Thanksgiving. I give thanks that I have my turkeys outside my window instead of on a platter!

November birds at early morning. While we sat at the dining table, outside the huge window we saw in the abelia bushes eight white-throated sparrows come to eat the tiny seeds, a phoebe alight upon a hickory limb and oblige us by sitting there the entire time we breakfasted, a hermit thrush on a higher limb who would not be outdone by the phoebe as a tree-sitter, a brown creeper walk up the hickory trunk, then fly down to the base of a dogwood to start up its trunk to

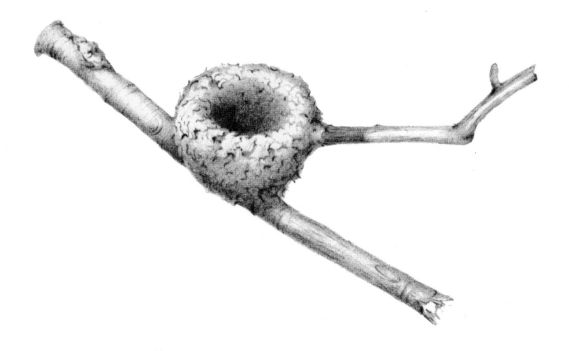

find insects in the bark. In the near-by pines was a flock of birds which through our field glasses we identified as both ruby- and golden-crowned kinglets. That list of birds was seen without effort as we dawdled over our fruit, cereal, and coffee; if our breakfast had been a larger meal, there would have been a longer list! As I cleared away the dishes I caught a glimpse of a blue jay, but, of course, blue jays are ever present, to many people hardly worth mentioning.

Ah, I remembered a certain morning shortly after Athos and I had moved to the rented house in the country. I recall that we were having breakfast on the screened porch when we heard blue jays screaming. We looked out to see a pair of jays swooping down at the three neighbor dogs; if invectives could kill, the dogs would have died instantly. Guessing at the cause of the commotion, Athos went outside to investigate. He returned with a baby jay that he had found helplessly fluttering on the ground.

The birdling cried a great deal, so we dubbed him "Baby Snooks," hoping that Fanny Brice would not object. It was apparent that he was not afraid of us, but cried because he was always hungry. Even when he could have eaten alone, the spoiled bird insisted that we feed him. He cuddled on our shoulders in an affectionate way, to reward us for letting him remain a baby despite his increasing size.

Snooks was mischievous and into everything from the day that he could leave his basket nest on the porch. He liked to untie shoestrings and poke little things into the shoes, and if we disturbed him he fussed at us and hurriedly retrieved his treasures to take elsewhere. Whenever he was shut on the porch, he battered frantically against the glass door, for he considered the entire house his property, and he resented being barred from the various places where he had hidden bits of pecans and prepared duck-food pellets. Crevices of chairs and the dirt of the potted plants were favorite hiding places for his hoarded food.

As he became older, he ate anything that was offered to him or that he could find. He was so quick in his thieving that once he grabbed a mouthful of poisonous white paint from the

Boat-tailed Grackle

palette before Athos could stop him. However, he did not object to being caught to have his mouth wiped out, and he obediently took olive oil and milk, which made him vomit the paint he had swallowed.

At first he had his drinking water from a soft paintbrush poked down his throat. But after he learned to drink from a glass or the dripping water faucet in the bathroom he would drink from nothing else, not even from the bowl in which he took his splashing bath every day.

Abandoning his basket, he selected a regular sleeping place on the shower rod in the bathroom. The metal was so slippery that Baby Snooks could not get a firm grip on the rod when he wanted to go to sleep standing on one foot, and kept sliding. Of course the bird spoke to Athos, who understood jay language, and he remedied the situation by tying a piece of felt on the rod. Snooks was placed on the cloth, found it to his liking, and promptly went to sleep on one foot.

As soon as Snooks began trying to make sounds other than his babyish squawks, he found that when Athos whistled three short notes he could answer in the exact tones. Snooks seemed to be pleased that he could imitate us perfectly, and wanted to keep it up. Then we whistled a certain melodic phrase with unvarying repetition and, to show his good intentions, Snooks tried his best to carry the long tune, although he rather garbled it. Later we became aware that he was imitating birdcalls that he heard, notably the caw of the crow.

The naughty-but-nice jay was the life of the party when we had guests. He liked anything that shone, and once he tugged at a proffered dime, pulled it from the hand, and hid it on top of a window. To discover how much weight Snooks could carry, we gave him a half dollar and he flew with it as effortlessly as he had with the dime. We had difficulty in getting it away from him, for he was playing a game and refused to be caught. He kept flying back to his favorite window-top, below which was a yawning floor grill for hot air, and if he dropped the fifty-cent piece it could not be retrieved. Athos used the ruse of dangling a piece of tinfoil in front of him, to make Snooks come to his shoulder and lose interest in the coin.

We found that we could take an article from him by waiting until he held it with his feet to peck at it and then, with a flourishing motion, pounce upon him in his confusion. He made a great to-do at our using unfair methods to trick him, although he did not bear a grudge long. There was a favorite game: we threw a thumb tack on the floor for him to grab, and our guests were alarmed as he appeared to swallow the tack. But we knew that he was merely holding it in his mouth until he was ready to tease us by dropping it on the floor to see if we could grab it before he could. He always won in the contest.

There was never a dull moment with Snooks around. One day when he was on the floor, Athos rapped the floor boards near him with his fingers. Immediately Snooks started prancing around the hand with crest up, tail fanned, slightly raising one wing and then the other, while tap-tapping his feet on the floor. As Athos continued to rap, Snooks kept up these queer capers for some time as though he were fighting, though without pecking at the hand. Since he was not old enough to know anything about love antics, we did not know why he behaved so ludicrously. The tap dancing became famous among our friends, although he had to be in the proper mood to perform for them.

After Snooks was fully able to care for himself, we took him outdoors one afternoon to set him free. Snooks made a short flight, chattering gaily, then returned to get some of the duck-food pellets that he knew were always in Athos's pocket. At that moment we regretted our hasty decision to let him go; it was imperative to our happiness that he remain with us a while longer.

Athos started toward the house with Snooks on his shoulder.

Suddenly there was a flash of blinding lightning, followed by deafening thunder! Snooks dashed off wildly, frightened out of his wits. He was out of sight in a jiffy, and no amount of whistling could recall him from the woods. Rain poured. During the ensuing hours, we felt wretched about our pet's being out for the first time under such adverse conditions; the poor little orphan of the storm would not know what to do to protect himself.

As darkness descended, Athos went out in the rain for one last attempt at whistling, in the hope that Snooks was somewhere near to hear. No bird came. There was no sound save the pattering of raindrops on the roof. We abandoned all hope of ever seeing Snooks again, and, to get our minds off our loss, we turned on the reading lamp and settled down to the evening newspaper.

Suddenly I saw Athos look up from the paper with a fixed stare of attention. He was on the alert about something, but what? Only the pattering of the rain—but no, there was another sound, as though someone was tap-tapping on the window-pane.

We looked out into the darkness and saw something fluttering there. Athos rushed to open the door and the bird flew to him! Snooks chattered

excitedly to be home, and I used baby-talk to him, and Athos stroked him. We were a family happily reunited.

Although wet to the skin, the bedraggled pet demanded his supper; he was so wet that he could hardly fly. After he had eaten, I hated the thought of Snooks going to bed soaking wet, and he had the same thought. He flew onto the lamp shade, where he knew that the electric bulb gave out heat, fluffed out his pitifully wet feathers, turned this way and that, and dried himself as effectively as if he had been in sunshine.

From that time, every morning we let him out the door to explore the wonderful world. Should it rain, he hurried back to us, but eventually he learned to find shelter outdoors. He did not stray far from the house, and we could hear him singing most of the time. As we walked in the adjacent woods, Snooks followed overhead in the trees, occasionally alighting on our shoulders and carrying on an animated conversation with us. He attended the feeding and care of the ducks, carrying away mouthfuls of duck-pellets for future reference.

He would fly to the door to tell us in jay language when he wanted it opened for him—presto! During the hot summer days he preferred to remain inactive in the cool shade of the indoors, until about four o'clock, when he would indicate that he wanted to go out to play until sunset. If he was not let out when he wanted to go, he whined, fussed, and fumed, and everyone was thoroughly miserable.

Snooks used the brook to take his baths, but when thirsty he returned to the house to drink out of a glass. He was so busy outdoors, flying, playing, and exploring, that he evidently did not hunt his food, and, when he came indoors, he fluttered his wings and opened his mouth wide, as a fledgling does, to let us know that he was ravenously hungry. He was a spoiled brat, but it was our privilege to indulge him as much as we chose.

The other birds shunned him. Once a determined female hummingbird carried on a one-sided fight with Snooks for half an hour—a tiny skyrocket—plaguing him until he came crying to the house to be rescued from her pestering. After many trials, he persuaded some young red-headed woodpeckers to frolic with him among the trees.

As Snooks was friendly and afraid of no person, our constant fear was that someone would shoot him, and whenever we heard gunshots in the vicinity we called him into the house. One morning we saw a man beating with a stick at the bushes alongside the road. Snooks had been thereabouts the last time we had heard from him, and, afraid that the bird might have tried to perch on the man's shoulder, we whistled frantically for him. The man went on his way and we hurried to search in the bushes to see if Snooks had been wounded or killed there. We found no trace of him.

To our relief, he returned late in the day. He was very hungry and tired, yet chattered happily with us. We had no proof that the man had hit at Snooks, but that was the only explanation we could think of for the prolonged absence of our pet. If he had been thus frightened, afterwards he showed no signs of being afraid of people. Our friends lavished affection on him, and I am convinced that all who knew Baby Snooks had a change of heart toward blue jays in general.

As time went on, he got into the company of other blue jays and would fly off with them for an entire day. He returned only at sunset: being a creature of habit, he wanted his supper and his shower-rod perch when darkness came. One night he spent out, but early the next morning we heard him at the door crying to be admitted and fed. After this taste of night life, he began to stay out more and more; yet he always returned in the morning. He took longer day trips, leaving our woods sometimes out of hearing range of our whistle. We could hear him in the distance calling that he was coming home, and it was a thrilling sight to see the gorgeous blue jay glide in for a perfect landing on our outstretched hands. It was gratifying to us to know that, with all the jays and the jolly times he had outdoors, he continued to be loyal to us, even seemed to crave our company. He could have forgotten us, but he chose to be faithful and companionable with the people who had raised him.

One evening he did not appear, nor the next. We whistled for him in vain, although we were not unduly alarmed over his absence. For days we awaited nightfall or eagerly listened for his cries in the morning. But he never returned.

Had he been the victim of a gun? Or had the other jays finally persuaded him to join their company permanently? We never knew, but we prayed that it was the latter. Every time we see or hear a jay, we wonder.

Morning sounds bring certain memories to me.

A moment ago I was pondering what bird or birds I wished next to write about. There are so many orders, then families, down to the lists of species, that a person would be staggered by the enormity of the subject unless some individual bird settled the question, as right now the call "killy-killy-killy" of an eastern sparrow hawk passing overhead settled the matter. Just as I

selected a specific blue jay to write about from among the numerous jays of our close acquaintance, now I wish to speak of a pet sparrow hawk, one of the sweetest, most affectionate creatures we have known.

We had not lived long in the rented country place when a telephone call summoned us to a house to get a sparrow hawk that two boys had caught. The boys put him into a makeshift cage in which we were to carry him home. That night, upon our arrival home, Athos reached into the back of the dark car to get the cage. He found to his surprise that the hawk had got out and was sitting on the seat, exactly in the manner of a human passenger. He made no objection to Athos's picking him up to carry him into the living room. In the light we discovered why he was so tame: his talon tips had been neatly clipped, explaining to us that he had been raised by someone, then had either escaped outdoors or been released voluntarily. He perched on our hands as though long accustomed to handling, evidencing no fear of us or of Yama.

At first we kept the little falcon in the house. We wanted to handle him a great deal, watch him all day, and Athos wished to paint his portrait. His size, eleven inches long, made him look like a toy. His general colors, cinnamon-rufous, gray, black and white with intricate markings, were pleasing to me; but what appealed to me most were his large, deep brown eyes.

To be sure, his eyes were keen, ever watchful, but even the projecting bony shield over the eyes could not give this pet the fierce and domineering expression of other hawks; his eyes had the same lovely quality as those of a doe.

Baby Snooks and the hawk romped together over the house. The jay tried to get the meat that was offered to the hawk, and often succeeded. When the hawk had had his fill, he would hide bits of meat, and Snooks took pleasure in stealing his treasures. The two birds indoors were about equal in flying, for the hawk was handicapped in flight because of the cramping space of the interior. Snooks's presence alleviated the boredom that the hawk must have felt, for Snooks was a great tease. We thought they were compatible, despite their difference in orders, until the day came when the hawk must have had enough of Snooks's foolishness, and wanted to teach him a lesson. In flight, he caught Snooks's tail and pulled out many of the feathers. Snooks's feelings were hurt, and he avoided the hawk thereafter.

Still people persist in calling blue jays "such mean birds." Well, hawks are "mean" also. We watched our sparrow hawk closely while Zulu was in a room with him, and never once did the bird of prey attack the marmoset. The environment was artificial, certainly, but it was interesting to observe these creatures arbitrarily thrown together.

Eventually we put the hawk into the large outdoor aviary. At once he was comfortable in his new quarters, not minding that other large birds shared his home. He appropriated a small dead tree put there for his perching place, which gave him a vantage point from which he could see all that was going on about him. In lieu of a hollow tree trunk in which to sleep, Athos placed a deep basket on a post in which he could have security for the night.

At mating season the hawk arranged and rearranged leaves, grasses, and small sticks in the basket to make a perfect nest, and called to lady friends to come to share his home. Then he began taking his pieces of meat into the basket, calling to the lady birds that he could feed them as well. Finally one heeded his call but she could not get inside the aviary; so Athos trapped her. However, she was wildly frightened at being closed in, for she had been accustomed to great open spaces, and, since the male could not induce her to be happy, we had to release her.

The hawk was particularly fond of Athos. When he saw his master come from the house, he raced to the door of the aviary to welcome Athos as he came inside. If he was hungry, he took the proffered meat immediately and flew to his perch to eat it; but if he had no appetite, he delighted in making believe he was striking. He was very gentle while indulging in this play and never once hurt Athos. He liked to alight upon Athos's head, grab with his talons a lock of hair to hold firmly, then, with his hooked bill, peck at the lock. Or he would sit on Athos's shoulder, gently nibbling at Athos's ear, the while making a soft chirping sound of contentment. He liked me well enough to perch on my hand as long as I remained in the aviary alone, but morning, noon, and evening Athos was his real playmate.

A day came when, as Athos was closing the aviary door, the sparrow hawk slipped out. He was free! He went from treetop to treetop, exploring and enjoying himself. No amount of calling from Athos or luring him with food could fetch him. Once when he was on a low limb, Athos placed a ladder against the tree trunk and reached for the hawk—who that instant flew away! The rest of the day he stayed in our vicinity, and we had to build up a philosophy that our pet was gone forever from our hands. As darkness came, he was nowhere to be seen.

We had settled down to the reading of the newspaper by the lamp when we heard something at the window—a pecking or striking of wings! We went outside and, almost as when Baby Snooks returned to us, the hawk flew to the door of the house! But he did not want to be let in; he had only come to tell us something. The little fellow flew directly to the aviary with us following him quickly. He waited until the door was opened, flew inside and to his basket nest for the night. He had had his outing, but when the day was over he, a creature of habit, wanted his usual security.

One day a pigeon in the aviary decided that she wanted that basket for her own nest, and took it without the sparrow hawk's putting up a fight. He moved to a small barrel that had a hole cut in it. Later the pigeons even took the barrel for nesting; so the hawk had to move under the shelter of the little house in the aviary. We had read somewhere of sparrow hawks going after pigeons, but ours ignored them, just as he ignored Snooks when he came into the aviary at feeding time. Perhaps our hawk was too well fed to bother about attacking other birds.

Little boys obligingly caught grasshoppers for the hawk, and he would take his favorite food from their hands. But he never really liked a stranger or dog, other than Yama, to approach his aviary, and would set up a "killy-killy-killy" alarm at the sight of either. All right, he would let people take his photograph and not be frightened of flash bulbs, but he wanted Athos close by to protect him. No, he would not show off for company. He allowed no one except me to see him play with Athos.

When we moved him to the aviary of our sanctuary, he was at home in it right away, for his beloved couple were near him to see that all was well. Often we brought him into the house for a change of environment. This he liked in the daytime, but he wanted to go to his aviary roost at night. In my mind's eye, right now I can see him sitting on a window curtain-rod watching everything we do, finding interest in our activities.

After four years, alas, there came a day when he did not feel well. We went to all sorts of trouble to secure freshly killed rodents and grasshoppers to feed him during the following weeks, instead of giving him store meat. As he continued to get worse, we thought he might improve if he had freedom outdoors. But he had little interest in flying about, returned to Athos, and seemed to prefer being in his safe aviary. We fondled him for hours, and it comforted him considerably not to be left alone in his illness. He was in Athos's hand when his last breath came, and peacefully, quietly, he slipped over the border.

I shall never forget Athos holding that lifeless bird in his hand, gently stroking it, speechless at the loss of his little playmate. But to us, whenever we hear a sparrow hawk, our pet lives again in memory. This morning he has been alive for me.

Yesterday, a November Sunday, Athos and I drove seventy miles to see my parents in Rome. Under a gray sky, through a wintry landscape, and along a road with which we were so familiar that it would have held little interest for us had we not enjoyed seeing the birds along the way. I reflected that it was not so many years ago that I would not have seen any of the birds, and such a morning ride would have been blank for me.

In other years, would I have known what a butcher bird was, or the purple grackles, or the meadow larks? Would I have been delighted to note that the slate-colored juncoes had returned south? Certainly I would not have exclaimed with pleasure at seeing twenty or thirty southern crows on newly plowed ground. In former years, had I seen crows, probably I would have said, "Who gives a hoot about crows? Noisy, colorless, dratted thieves!"

We stopped the automobile to watch the crows, at first for sheer joy at the sight; then I realized that their physical characteristics and their behavior were being impressed upon Athos's mind as he made mention of details. Many persons have asked the question, "How long does it take Menaboni to paint a bird picture?" As we sat on the road watching the busy scene, I knew that a picture was being conceived; before long it was complete, and nothing remained to be done save to let the mental picture flow from the artist's fingers onto the canvas. And this morning I see that, without apparent effort, the crow is magically appearing on canvas where only a few minutes ago was nothing at all. That automobile ride yesterday had not been blank for Athos. He

had lifted out of the general scene a detail in nature which he desired to reproduce, or, to put it another way, the creative work had been done yesterday, and merely the execution follows now.

I wish that I could give a delightful word picture of a crow we had once. I shall have to record facts, but, in so doing, I must say that that crow was not typical of crows in general. Even the fact that two boys caught him on the ground proved that he was not normal; they said that the parent birds had tried to talk him into flying up, but the young bird could only flutter helplessly. We were glad that the boys had brought him to us, for we had long wanted this species. Then, too, we anticipated an amusing pet, because so many people had written about crows as most intelligent birds.

He was already quite a large bird, with huge bill, legs, and feet. Too young to have the fine metallic sheen of the adults, our crow was rusty black, with only a hint of the changeable blue and purplish iridescence that would come later upon his feathers. The eyes were grayish-blue, and, as he blinked in the sunshine, the filmy third eyelids were useful to keep the glare out of his pupils.

The fledgling perched on our fingers without protesting. When he was placed on a wooden box edge, he stayed there, apparently content to be on the screened porch. He must have been considerably upset by the ordeal of being with people, though, for within half an hour he gave up his breakfast of whole kernels of green corn.

After we surmised that his nerves were calmed, we gave him a meal, topped off with fresh strawberries. He drank water from a spoon, and I chuckled as I said, "Here we are again with a spoon-fed baby!"

We wanted a photograph of him, and the bird did not object to riding upon a finger, nor did he try to escape from us when we went outdoors. The sunshine made him very hot, however, and soon his bill flew open as he began to pant. Previously Athos had told me that birds do not

perspire in the ordinary way. Now I discovered that panting with open bill controls their body temperature. We compensated the crow for his discomfort by taking him to the house for another meal, and he made gurgling guttural sounds while being fed. Then he took a siesta. For a new bird, he was easily managed.

After several days, we noticed that the screened porch enclosure was too small a space in which to give him the opportunity to learn to fly well, and we took him to the aviary. What a poor reception the other birds gave him! The wild turkeys "put-put-put"-ed, the mallards squawked, the sparrow hawk shrilled "killy-killy-killy," and others protested as vigorously. When they came menacingly near him, he told them crossly that he did not care for them either! However, when Athos had remained in the aviary for some time, with the crow sitting still on his perch, the others soon understood that there was nothing to fear from him and unanimously decided to ignore him.

In the aviary his disposition changed. While he had not objected to our handling before, now he sought a high branch beyond the reach of our hands. While we were near, he did not fly down for the food that was left for him. We did not want a wild bird with which to contend, so after a few days of this standoffish behavior, Athos caught him to bring him indoors again. On the porch he became as gentle and easy to handle as before.

The summer heat made the crow suffer; he sat immovable for hours, panting, and he drank a great deal of the water that we offered to him often. One afternoon, out of sympathy, I transferred him to the coolest room in the house, the bathroom. He was so relieved that we decided that only his mornings should be spent on the porch, and the rest of the time in the bathroom.

When we felt that he would always let us feed him, he was again taken to the outdoor pen. By handling him often there, and bringing him to the house at night, we kept him tame. Tame,

Canada Goose

yes, but unresponsive. Patiently we waited for him to start showing some startling signs of intelligence. Certainly he was a dullard while young, not living up to the reputation crows have of being smart, mischievous, and very entertaining. Most of the time he just sat—like a bump on a log.

We decided that the wisest course with this bird was to release him when he was able to fly well, so that he might develop a higher mentality than he was evidencing in our hands. When freed, he stayed in our trees, without going far away. He reverted to wildness, not coming to our hands for proffered food even while crying that he was very hungry, and not eating the food regularly left on top of the aviary until we walked away. Day after day he stayed in the trees, not doing anything in particular, simply sitting there stupidly.

We had used our best efforts in his behalf, but the human efforts had not been enough for this bird, for one evening Athos found him lying on top of the aviary wire, dead. We concluded that he must have been sick from the very beginning and we had not known it. He had not been responsible for his seeming low mentality.

We were sorry that our bird had not had a long life span and enjoyed living. Perhaps we had prolonged his life beyond the time nature had allotted him. We hope that some other time we shall have a crow that will be a wonderful pet.

At any rate, I have no prejudice against crows; indeed, I have a great sympathy and admiration for them. I am aware that they eat some corn to worry the farmer, but I have seen statistics which prove that crows, because they are omnivorous, help that same farmer to be rid of insect pests.

I have had fun watching crows chasing hawks, deviling them to distraction, and, on the other hand, seen a kingbird worry a crow into leaving a territory. Time and again I have seen crows hastening to help their brothers upon hearing the call for help. When I hear excited crows cawing, I know that I must go outdoors to watch an important and dramatic event.

If for nothing else, I am thankful that crows are responsible for comic relief to a winter landscape. Yesterday, for example, the crows were upon the freshly broken ground eating any insects they could turn up, right under the nose of the "scarecrow" while it futilely waved its empty coat sleeves.

Fast flying in V formation, and at a great height, uttering a resonant honking, Canada geese on their way south form one of the marvelous sights of autumn.

This morning a Canada gander came to us from Montana.

Outside my window I see him and the goose taking a nap. They are side by side, alike in color; each stands on one foot, and their long velvety black necks are curved back so that the heads can be tucked under their wings. It gives me satisfaction to see that the gander has made himself so at home that he is undisturbed by thirteen mallards a couple of feet distant, sleeping in the same manner, and a little farther away a wild turkey squatting on the ground dozing.

My thoughts go back to the year we visited Blue Springs Farm and were awed when we saw the thousands of these largest of wild geese that had been raised there. It followed naturally that our good friend there should kindly give a pair to us.

The dignified birds made themselves at home in the aviary of the rented country home, but manifested a wariness that never left them until we brought them to live in our sanctuary. I remember the time we transported them in our automobile, with me at the steering wheel, and Athos and Ike each holding a goose in his arms. When the birds were set on the ground here, where they were free to go wherever they chose over the acreage, they began displaying their true characteristics.

They had a certain routine to follow every day. Upon awakening, and in no hurry, they ambled down to the gate to graze until they heard Athos close the door of the house. That meant he was going to feed the birds, and, honking that they were coming, they hurried up the hill to get their share of the grains. Following that, there was a period of rest before they sauntered to the valley to find succulent greens, then up to the house to see again what was going on, for they seemed not to want to miss anything around the sanctuary center of activity. In the afternoon they went along the path to the pool for bathing. Back, along a different route, they came nibbling at herbage along the way, to a supper of grain, then off to sleep among the rocks on the hill beside the house. Day after day this regular routine was followed.

However, when the biological urge to nest possessed them, their routine changed. They searched over the land for a suitable nesting site, ending up by selecting a spot behind a tree up the hill fifty feet from the pool. The place where the brook curved became the dividing line of their exclusive territory, and the gander vigilantly watched over it, ever ready to fight off intruders. The turkeys needed no second warning, nor did the mallards, that they were to keep away from the hissing gander. Yama was bolder and did not run away, but waited until the hitherto docile gander rushed at him with lowered head, outstretched neck, and ruffled feathers; when it became apparent that the hissing was not menacing enough, the gander rushed at Yama, caught his hair and gave him a blow with his wing. The dog pulled loose, loped to safety, and never again stepped across the brook in nesting time.

At that time the geese would not come to the house to be fed, and Athos took grain to place beside the pool, where the gander suffered his presence. He did not like mine, however, and, in cowardice, I walked behind Athos for protection. Once I turned my back to walk away from the infuriated gander; he ran after me and I did not jump across the brook fast enough to escape having a nip of the bill upon my bare leg. After that, in going away from him, I walked backwards, using a technique of frustrating the gander by waving a stick from side to side close to the ground, or even waving my empty hands near the ground. Athos did not have to resort to these methods of protection, for the gander, although threatening him, even once or twice catching hold of his trousers and holding fast, sensed that Athos had no fear of him. Athos was deliberate in his slow movements and talked calmly to the gander, who seemed to know what Athos was saying.

I had the laugh on Athos once, although he did not think there was anything funny about the whole thing. One day he bravely decided that he would go up to see the nest with the goose on it. The gander protested vigorously, telling Athos in plain language not to proceed up the hill. As Athos continued, the affront was too much for the gander; he rushed suddenly, grabbed Athos's trousers and held fast to the cloth with bulldog tenacity, then with powerful blows of the wing elbows, he beat Athos's knees viciously again and again. Athos had to use all his strength to free himself. He made a hasty, inglorious retreat, limping down the hill. My laughing did not improve his hurt! However, I became solicitous when he limped for a week. Never again did Athos attempt to go to the nest. Decidedly, a Canada gander is not to be trifled with during nesting season.

It was fortunate that we knew what to do. Once, during a party, a photographer, whom we had not warned, walked into the valley ahead of us. Suddenly we saw him running back frantically, almost knocking down some of the ladies with us, who scattered pell-mell. The gander was half running, half flying after the man. He fell sprawling on the ground, and the gander jumped on top of him. Double-quick in any emergency, Athos went to the rescue; he lunged at the gander, gathering the large bird in his arms to hold the wings to the bird's body, and in the nick of time prevented the man from getting a beating that he would never have forgotten.

(Afterwards we remembered that the man instinctively had had the presence of mind as he fell to hold aloft his precious camera!)

The gander was very gentle and caressing to the goose when she came from her nest to eat and to splash in the pool with him. They were exceedingly happy—if people would stay away. We did for the most part keep away from them, so they could have the privacy they needed for their domestic affairs.

We did not know exactly when the eggs were laid, but we guessed at the day on which we thought the goose had begun the sitting. For twenty-eight days—for a week longer and still another week—we waited for the appearance of goslings. Surely the time was up, was overdue. What was wrong?

One morning Athos found the goose lying dead beside the pool. Alas, we had not known that she had a malady, which had caused a big open wound in her back. The gander was still honking, still protecting her. The three eggs, carefully covered with soft body feathers in the nest made of sticks and lined with goose-down, were infertile.

For days the gander mourned, grieved, and called for the goose to come back. We sympathized greatly with him and from out of town we ordered a new goose, in the hope that the two would like each other. Suppose they did not, then what?

From the crate we took the newcomer, who immediately began eating. The gander fell in love with her at first sight and started making affectionate overtures to her. Five minutes later he urged her to go walking with him, apparently

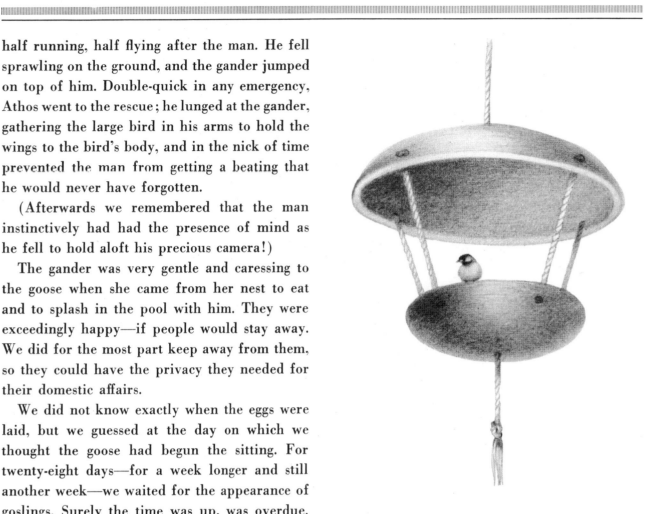

thrilled to take her on a tour of her new home grounds. She accepted him as naturally as he accepted her.

A pair of Canada geese are inseparable; if by chance one goes ten feet distant from the other and out of sight, there is a great clamor until they are reunited.

Athos and I have been on two wild-goose chases —literally. One autumn we waited a bit too long to cut the primary feathers on one wing of each bird to prevent them from flying away; this was due to the fact that we knew that new feather quills have to be quite long before they can be cut or else they will bleed, and it is very difficult to know just when to cut the feathers. One dawn we heard the geese flying away, honking.

The farmer across the road came to tell us that the gander had landed in his yard. Athos went there to catch the bird, bring him home,

Pileated Woodpecker

and clip the wing feathers. There was no guessing where the goose had flown. All day we hunted for her over the countryside. The gander called for the goose to return, called incessantly with his strident, carrying voice. At sunset we saw her alight on the road in front of the sanctuary gate. After Athos opened the gate, she walked up the driveway, calling to her mate. When they had their reunion, the gander pecked at her!

The next year the gander did not leave, for his wing feathers had been cut in time, but the goose flew away before Athos could catch her to clip her feathers. Again we searched, again the gander summoned her, and in midmorning we found her endeavoring to find a way through the fence. Yama helped us direct her to the gate.

Two more nestings were made in the exact spot by the tree, but never a gosling appeared. Since the second goose did not have fertile eggs, we began to wonder if something was wrong with the gander. They seemed to have an ideal life, except for migrating as would be normal; they had plenty of space in which to roam, food to make them fat, water in which to swim and bathe, no enemies, plenty of interesting things happening to prevent boredom, and, if they lacked anything else to do, they could come to the glass doors of our house to peer in at us.

They had one bad habit. They resented mallard ducklings underfoot, and when they could catch one with their bills, they shook it vigorously, often killing one. This caused a great commotion from the mama-duck, other ducks and drakes entering into the fray. Yama tried to "break it up, break it up," without hurting geese or ducks. And the Menabonis rushed out of the house to save a duckling from being killed if they could get there in time, or brought indoors many a wounded or stunned duckling to nurse. Often we had to pen the geese when there were ducklings about.

Unsolvable mysteries sometimes occur. One morning not long ago, after the gander had seemed perfectly well the night before, Athos found him dead. There was no sign of any violence, nothing on the exterior to indicate what had caused death, nor, when Athos examined the interior of the body, could he find any unhealthy condition; we never determined the cause of death. But Athos did find that the reproductive organs were not normal, in fact almost nonexistent. This was undoubtedly the answer to the question of why there had been so many infertile eggs.

The goose was bereft, crying every hour of every day. I started writing over the country for a mate for her—very difficult to find in November, when the young birds of the past spring broods have not yet manifested whether they are males or females—and no game-farm breeder would separate a mated pair. After many weeks, the goose became reconciled to being single, and either stayed close by the house for our company or went about with the mallards. But I persisted in letter writing, and at last we found a game-farmer in Montana who had an unmated gander to send to us.

This morning, when we introduced the two birds to each other, they acted very indifferent, yet readily accepted the fact that they were to be together.

Will there be goslings the next nesting season? Is this the proper gander?

CHAPTER FIVE

Some women like to collect diamonds, others get increasingly expensive antiques; and some men want a string of horses, or fluorescent stones—all of us yearn to possess what we have set our hearts on getting. Sometimes collecting is only a passing fancy, but with Athos, from early childhood, his interest has been in the acquiring of birds and more birds. Since I have learned the joys of collecting, I have had an insatiable desire to add to my bird list. It will never be as long as my husband's, but he devotes himself to helping me, and we appreciate the fact that we have this interest together.

To read of birds I have not yet encountered drives me into a frenzy of desire to see them. Today I have been reading a book, sent to us by a friend made through correspondence, about South African birds. I am filled with frustration because I am not this minute packing and scurrying to get on the next ship that sails to South Africa. On the other hand, the man in Johannesburg wishes that he could see the birds that are my everyday companions. We cannot be everywhere and doing everything at once; therefore, I calm myself and decide that I am grateful for what I have right here.

The last bird added to my bird list was a blue-winged warbler, and the one before that was a yellow-throated vireo. I wonder how many people know these two birds? They are not common sights for Athos and me, yet are ordinary perhaps to bird students in other parts of the country. I know that within our continental limits are dozens of species still to be seen by me. For that matter, around my own Atlanta, I have not met up with a prothonotary warbler, over which one local bird lady, when reporting a field trip, exclaimed, "We saw a prothonotary warbler who thrilled us all spring—and summer too!"

An ornithologist from Philadelphia came to Atlanta last year for his first visit and, with us, saw his first summer tanager. It was a common bird to us, but made him say in ecstasy, "Now I have lived!" Was he content with "living" in the past tense? There is no satisfying an ardent bird student, as a stamp collector is never content with what he has; there was still an hour before dark, and that man eagerly searched for his next new bird. Happily he added to his list a pileated **woodpecker**.

Collecting new names on our bird list is not the prime interest of Athos and me; we want to familiarize ourselves with the characteristics of each new species and its natural habitat. Indeed, this is of utmost importance to a naturalist-artist; Athos must know each subject intimately before he can paint its portrait. There is no way to learn about birds at first hand except to go search for them.

When first I set out upon the new adventure with Athos, we found that our friends took a sudden interest in the quest for birds. Had we not had a definite purpose in going on jaunts, we should never have bothered to seek out the fields, swamps, hills, and valleys, and would never have seen all the scenic beauties that lay outside the city limits.

Our equipment for collecting was nothing more than field glasses and a field guidebook on birds, should we chance upon unknown species. We knew we should dress in comfortable hiking clothes of somber colors, the older the better. We went with only a couple of companions each time, for a large group frightens birds, and we had to talk softly and walk casually. We allowed ourselves hours for each field trip, for birds cannot be seen in a hurry.

From personal experience and observation, I

believe there are no happier persons than those who are intent upon collecting nature data. And each person should make a beginning of his collection in his own "back yard." Of course he may branch out, go farther afield, perhaps decide to specialize in one subject, but the more he learns the more he knows lies in wait for him in his original back yard. After we moved to the country, we learned that we did not have to drive miles away to see the birds. Under a woodpile was our very own Carolina wren nesting; a brown-headed nuthatch had a nest in a stump hole; a red-eyed vireo had her nest in a dogwood; a crested flycatcher came often to perch on a limb at our back door; there was a redstart in our woods—and every discovery added to our pleasure as well as knowledge. Now, when I am in the city, I have a deeper appreciation for the birds that are right there for the persons who place a high value upon them.

The preceding summer I was summoned to a city apartment to get a young sparrow hawk that a lady had found upon her window sill. She liked him well enough for his appearance, giving him the name of "Joseph-with-the-coat-of-many-colors," and she did not object to solving the problems of feeding him, but she knew that he should not be kept in a cage that would prevent him from growing into a healthy adult; so she had telephoned us to come get him to raise. I told her of the joys of having a sparrow hawk, and asked why she did not herself wish to keep him free in her apartment until he was old enough to be liberated? Oh, no, Joseph was not housebroken and would streak her furniture and draperies with droppings. I brought Joseph to my own house, where he could leave his "calling cards" all over my furniture, draperies, and rugs! Furnishings could be cleaned or replaced, but nothing could ever replace the fun and additional bird data we got from Joseph until we released him.

The last estimated population of Atlanta was 330,000 people, but I daresay only a fraction of that figure knows certain of our birds—for instance, the phoebe, red-bellied woodpecker, brown creeper, black and white warbler, broad-winged hawk, purple finch. Perhaps they do not know that hermit and gray-cheeked thrushes even exist; have missed the joys of seeing the diminutive golden-crowned and ruby-crowned kinglets; and have they seen a killdeer, woodcock, Wilson's snipe, and wood peewee? Few know the difference between a wood thrush and a brown thrasher, as I once did not, even though these occur in great numbers here. In giving bird talks to over a hundred organizations in Atlanta to date, I have found that my audiences look blank when I mention the majority of the above-mentioned birds. "Gold is where you find it," and these people have not looked for it. I know that first I must collect my own native birds, appreciate them, and gain a background of knowledge about birds in general before I trek off to South Africa to see the "blue crane, red-billed hornbill, crowned guineafowl, white-fronted bee eater," and all those other birds which seem so glamorous in the book I studied today. It behooves me to see my first prothonotary warbler right here! In books on American birds, he sounds as glamorous as a South African one. I recall a time when I wondered what made farmer folk seek glamour in the little Georgia town of Cave Springs, the inhabitants of Cave Springs come to my town of Rome, Romans go to Atlanta, Atlantans go to New York, New Yorkers go to Europe. Where on earth did the Europeans go? I found out later that Europeans wanted to go to New York. After they got there, they wanted to come to Atlanta, and when in Atlanta they wanted to move out to a country farm! At least, this is what happened to Athos from Europe, and to me too. I found later that Emerson had nicely summed it up: "Travelling is a fool's paradise. We owe to our first journeys the discovery that place is nothing. At home I dream that at Naples, at Rome, I can be intoxicated with beauty and lose my sadness. I pack my trunk, embrace my friends, embark on the sea and at last wake up in Naples, and there beside me is the stern Fact, the sad self, unrelenting, identical, that I had fled from."

It so happens that Athos and I are lucky people, able to do exactly what pleases us most. It pleases us to stay right here now, preparing this book to share our personal birds with all who wish them. And who knows, the friend in South Africa may enjoy our birds as much as we have enjoyed his native birds; our book shall do the traveling, as other books have traveled to us from far places. We can't distribute a collection of diamonds, antiques, horses, or fluorescent stones, but anyone who wants them can have our birds!

One never knows what will appear unexpectedly. In the summer we have our suppers outdoors in our sanctuary, and I recall several consecutive evenings when I heard a peculiar catlike cry from across the road in the thicket along the creek. Finally I mentioned it to Athos, who began concentrating upon the call. Decidedly it was not a cat; undoubtedly it was that of a bird, but what bird? We thought it might be an owl, but the word descriptions in our books did not seem to fit our particular mysterious bird. If it was an owl, it was not one with which we were familiar in Atlanta. Then, one dusk, the sound was in our sanctuary. Stealthily, scarcely breathing, we stalked the bird whose call gave its location. It was wary of our approach and flew away, but not too fast for us to see that it was truly an owl. However, it left too quickly for us to see identification marks. We looked in all our books at owl pictures, but could not be sure of what we had seen. Another evening it came to our sanctuary and we had a perfect view of it: a short-eared owl. Nor was it our only view, for the bird came often after that, apparently having learned not

to be afraid of us. We thought it must be nesting across the road, but we never invaded its privacy. The bird left us in late autumn.

From a scientific standpoint, it was unfortunate that we did not go into the study of that single bird from all angles, ascertain if it really nested, and note every detail about it. To us it had been merely another owl on our bird list and enjoyable to see, but it should have been more to us than that, for we did not know at the time what a find we had. It was six months later that the short-eared owl was reported as a record for Atlanta, the first time on the official list. I am glad that we did not kill ours and, by having a specimen, prove that we had seen it earlier, for the one which was added to the official list might have been the same one, or possibly an offspring. But we were provoked at ourselves for having muffed our opportunity to add something to ornithology beyond another name on our personal list. It is in countless methods of gathering bird data that all the books on ornithology have come into being.

Perhaps this is a good time to bring up the subject of the excellent bird books that are available. There are several standard works that bird lovers swear by, but no one book tells everything about all the birds, for this is an impossibility as in every other branch of science. However, anyone interested in the subject should have several books on hand to use when he sees an unknown bird; for it should be looked up in a book immediately, and its name and a description of its characteristics found, in order that it may become indelibly stamped upon the memory. I am amazed at the number of people who profess to love birds dearly, who feed them and try to protect them from hazards, yet who do not have a single book for reference. Athos and I have countless bird books overflowing to the attic, to say nothing of all the magazines, monographs, bulletins, etc., on the subject. But sometimes we look in vain for some piece of information we need to satisfy our curiosity and add to our fund of knowledge.

This brings up the matter of why it is necessary not only to read about birds, but to go in search of the answers to many questions we personally desire to know. I will give an illustration. Remember that early in this book I described a ruby-throated hummingbird nest, and in part I quote: "covered externally with lichens fastened with spiderwebs." Ah, but how were the spiderwebs collected by the hummingbird and fabricated into that wee nest? Perhaps someone has written about it, but our particular books did not tell us. At long last we saw a female hummingbird about her task. She flew deliberately into spiderwebs, got them all over her head feathers, returned to her almost completed nest, rubbed her head against it to dislodge the spiderwebs from her feathers, and then with her bill placed the webs where she wanted them among the lichens she went to fetch piece by piece.

One problem solved leads to another that we wish to know the answer to. The blue-gray gnatcatcher has a nest almost identical with that of a ruby-throated hummingbird, but larger, yet these two birds belong to entirely different orders of birds. Did the blue-gray gnatcatcher gather spiderwebs in the same manner? We eventually observed both male and female blue-gray gnatcatchers working at nest building, *and* they went about their business of gathering spiderwebs and lichens in the exact manner that the female ruby-throated hummingbird employed alone.

Then, too, we like to find examples that differ from the ordinary. For example, as I said earlier, the ruby-throated hummingbird generally nests on a tree limb fifteen to twenty-five feet up, but we had seen one at least a hundred feet up; and generally the blue-gray gnatcatcher nest is up twelve to thirty feet, but we have seen one seventy feet high, and still another about a hundred feet up. Such little examples of observation in nature have taught me not to make generalizations about people!

Collectors' items are strewn around, just waiting to be garnered. The books point out the path to them, but a book has no power to take a person physically by the arm and pull him down that path forcibly—or has it? I remember the time when I had been reading about the yellow-billed cuckoo, often called "rain crow," which I had not seen. If other persons had seen this bird, I wanted to see it also. I got up from my chair and went out into the woods. I wandered about, then finally sat on a boulder. I sat there for some time and there came to mind the work I was neglecting in my house. I knew I should have been galloping about trying to do the world's work, and I reproached myself for idling away the valuable hours. However, I thought, what do we work so hard to gain? Why do we have timesaving gadgets except to give us more leisure for our pursuit of happiness? Exactly *what* is of value? I was having a hot debate with myself when out of the corner of my eyes I saw a bird sitting on a limb three feet away from me. It was snowy white beneath, the bill was slightly downcurved, the wings were rufous—and I was actually seeing the yellow-billed cuckoo! How long had he calmly surveyed me? While I had been in a mental stew, he had come to me quietly. And I had kept faith with the author who had hoped to make me bestir myself to go out in search of my first yellow-billed cuckoo. We looked at each other for fully fifteen minutes, then he stole off silently and ghost-like through the woods. When I returned to my house, saw the book lying on the vacated chair, I spoke aloud to my friend the author: "Thanks for making me go outdoors."

The book's description of a yellow-billed cuckoo's voice gave a clue as to what to expect, but Athos and I could not fit any call in the wild with our secretive bird. It was not until a couple of years later that we saw a yellow-billed cuckoo with his throat quivering and his bill slightly open as he emitted the peculiar, indescribably rolling, croaking sound. We realized that we had heard that call dozens of times and had not associated it with a bird. Since then every summer we hear the call, and, although a whole season may pass without our sighting one of these hard-to-see birds, we know that yellow-billed cuckoos are near us.

Knowing that call was once of inestimable value to us. We had heard the birds calling in our woods and surmised that they were nesting near by. One day Athos stood still for an hour, trying in vain to locate the bird with the ventriloquial voice. Later he revisited the scene and heard it again, but this time he noted a peculiarity about it that made him wonder if it was a fledgling; the more he listened the more he was convinced that it was a young bird crying. He scanned each tree minutely, searched the thicket, and tried standing in different places to locate the elusive sound, but it was an impossibility to find the bird. He turned his attention then to the building of a stone wall there. Once he straightened up to rest his back and happened to glance above his head—there sat the baby cuckoo on a limb. It was where Athos must have looked, or rather overlooked, a dozen times during his fruitless search. From his observation of the young bird, Athos judged that it was too small to be normally out of the nest, so he gathered it into his hands. He tried to find the nest, but could

not. During those hours Athos had not seen or heard the parents, and evidently something had happened to them; in fact, that season we did not hear or see adults again.

When Athos arrived at the house with the fledgling perched on his finger, he called to me, "Come guess what I have." I had never seen such a baby bird, but it gave me great satisfaction to guess correctly, at the moment that Athos was ready to tease me about my ignorance of birds!

How to feed it? There I *was* ignorant. The books told us that this was one of the few species that eat the fuzzy tent caterpillars. For once we were glad that we had procrastinated in burning out the tent caterpillar nests from our wild cherry trees. And evenings Athos collected enough insects that were attracted to our windows by the electric light to supplement the food for the cuckoo. Of course our friends joked about how we were "cuckoo" to go to all that bother, but I noticed that quite a few of them collected insects to bring to our baby bird! We successfully raised the bird and many people saw him before we released him as an adult, so that thereafter they would know how to identify him. Once a person has seen a cuckoo he won't forget it.

Often male birds fight terrifically for a certain nesting territory. Once Athos observed two male indigo buntings having a battle royal, and in his swift flight one of them hit something and fell to the ground disabled. Athos brought him into the house for a few days to recover completely before turning him loose. I looked at this rich blue-plumaged bird, with his dusky wings and tail margined with blue. He was much smaller than a sparrow, and in my house an ornament of lively interest. I could not reconcile my thoughts to his being pugilistic to the extreme over possessing a hundred or two yards of nesting ground when there was so much space outdoors. But it was flattering to know that our sanctuary was so desirable that males coveted it for their homes.

75

One morning we heard the indigo bunting singing in our living room, and we knew that he was ready to go out upon his business of rearing a family. Later we located a female sitting upon her nicely made nest on wild bamboo, and a male was close by watching us to see that we should not harm his lady-love; we wondered which male this was—the victor in the fray or the one who had received the knockout blow and yet gone forth to create a family anyhow, not knowing that some person would tell of his disgrace.

Shortly after that we were driving at dusk, the time of poor visibility. We were going around a bad curve, through a railroad underpass that is famous as a location for automobile accidents. Suddenly Athos jammed on the brakes and the car swerved drunkenly. He pulled up by the curb, threw open his door, jumped out and started running back. My heart stood still in fear —what on earth? Dear God, keep an automobile from coming around that blind curve and hitting my husband! I started getting angry too—what dangers Athos sometimes exposes himself to! Well, sir, he had in that poor light seen an indigo bunting lying on the pavement and noticed a feeble movement of his body. He returned to me with the little bird lying senseless in his hand, but alive; no doubt another automobile would have finished off that bird's life had Athos not rescued it.

In our home the indigo bunting completely recovered and filled our days with one of the sweetest of melodies. He had the liberty of the whole house and became very tame. We gave him what we thought were the proper foods the year we kept him, but a curious thing happened with his spring molting. He started changing from his winter coat of brownish-gray into his blue breeding coloration, which was natural, but he never completely changed into blue before he got back into winter grays again. Not only did his coloration not come properly, but his feathers came

out frizzly. The biology of our pet was haywire, probably due to a deficiency in diet; so we turned him loose outdoors, in the hope that he would regain normalcy. He went away, so we never knew what the rest of his life history was.

Once in a blue moon an albino bird can be seen. Long ago in Florida, Athos had seen an albino tree swallow on the wing, and once a partially albino robin had been brought to us, but I had never seen a true albino and I wondered if I ever should see the rare sight. I did not give my unknown friends, made through my writing for publication, the credit that was due them, for if I brought birds to them, wasn't it the most logical supposition that they would bring birds to me? A telephone call came one day from strangers with this story: they had bluebirds nesting in a box on a dogwood tree, and the day before the young flew away they had peeked into the box to see two naturally colored youngsters and a pure-white one. They had taken out the albino fledgling and photographed it. That had been at Easter, and in due course the same pair of adults had built their second nest in another house-box in an elm a hundred feet distant from the first nest. When the babies were almost ready to fly, the people looked into the second nest, finding five youngsters, three of them albinos. Did the Menabonis wish to see them?

That June 12 Athos and I were very busy, but we dropped everything and immediately went to see the three white bluebirds with pink eyes. Athos lifted them onto the ground in the sunlight to photograph them as positive proof.

We had remarkable data to add to our personal collection, but we asked if we could bring others to see the unusual birds. Of course our new friends wanted to have others come, and we telephoned hastily to an ornithologically minded man, who, although he was at his office as tied up as businessmen are, rushed out to us with his motion-picture equipment. By the time he arrived, the parent birds had coaxed one albino

Killdeer

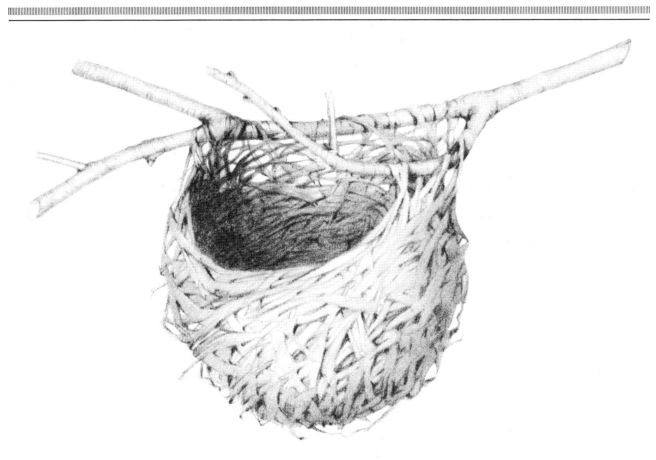

to come out of the box to start flying. We spent the rest of the day assisting our friend to get his colored motion pictures of the albino and his bluebird parents. He took pictures of them in all sorts of poses, especially feeding the young bird, proving beyond a shadow of a doubt that the white one belonged to bluebird parents. We few persons had personally witnessed the sight, but through the medium of movies many large audiences could see the little one who freakishly lacked pigmentation. It was our last opportunity to photograph the birds, for the next day all were gone.

Yes, those young birds disappeared, but the parents soon laid another clutch of eggs in the first birdhouse they had used on the dogwood tree. On July 28 the lady telephoned to us to bring more interested people to see five more fledglings, three of whom were albinos! Of the thirteen young birds of that season, seven were albinos. Scientists have enjoyed themselves explaining the whole thing, using a lot of mathe-

matics. I have enjoyed knowing that some people observed birds and, after having found something extraordinary, did not keep it to themselves but wanted a way, and found a way, of sharing it. And their story now appears in a book for more people to share!

Have you ever seen a bird "as naked as a blue jay"? I have; that is, it was almost nude. One day I drove up my driveway to the terrace in front of the house, and as I stopped the automobile, a voice called "Hello." I didn't see Athos or anyone about, and presumed that the greeting had come from around the corner of the house. "Hello" came again to me—from under the tulip tree at the side of the terrace. I looked in that direction and was startled, but had presence enough to say in return, "Why, hello there!" I was embarrassed as I walked toward an unclothed red macaw.

He did have head feathers and a few primary and tail feathers that he could not willfully pluck out himself. From the house Athos brought out the couple who owned Chou Chou, and who had brought him to us to have his portrait painted. Oh, no, they did not want him painted to look like the fright he was, but with his head to serve as a model, Athos could go to the zoo to study red macaws there for the rest of the plumage.

Pulling out his feathers hurt him, and as he did so he grunted with pain, but he liked the taste of the drop of blood that was at the bottom of the new quill. We promptly told the owners, "Deficiency in diet." It was the wrong thing to say, for both husband and wife were doctors and the wife had just completed an additional year of university study in diet work; they vowed that they had tried everything imaginable to give their macaw foods that would remedy any dietary deficiency. We concluded that the macaw had a perverted taste, and since the bird was brought to us for a couple of months' visit, Athos confidently, even boastfully said that he could and would break the bird of his bad habit. In time Athos found that he had not reckoned on a will power that would outmatch his! No matter what Athos did, the macaw continued to pluck out all the feathers he could as soon as new quills started appearing. Finally Athos had to admit defeat, much to the amusement of the owners.

Athos, to save his face, did outsmart Chou Chou in one way. Before coming to his present owners, Chou Chou had had a broken wing that had not set properly, and he was, therefore, unable to fly; but with his feet adapted to climbing (two toes forward and two at the back) and his powerful bill, he could get around remarkably well in spite of the inability to fly. His owners had brought along his stand, which consisted of a post with props, a tray on top for his food, and a perch. Whenever he wished, he could climb down to the floor to go chew out hunks of the furniture or have great fun sidling over to an unsuspecting person to take a nip at an

ankle. To prevent this from happening in the house, Athos tied around the post a lot of wadded newspapers, over which Chou Chou could not figure how to climb. He knew how to say many things in English but no curse words; however, in macaw language, he used blistering profanity. The newspaper barrier drove him into a frenzy of rage and he tore it to bits; when Chou Chou had rid himself of his obstacle and begun his descent, Athos tied another piece of wadded newspaper on the post, and Chou Chou screamed epithets at my husband. Driven to near-madness, Chou Chou started chewing the newspapers again. The real laugh was on *me*, for it was my job to clean the floor of paper tatters! I confess that I said some unladylike things and wondered what I had done to deserve to be married to an artist and have big birds in my house.

To carry Chou Chou about, we used a short length of broom handle, and happily he would step onto one end of it. Athos did this the first time, and did not pay attention to Chou Chou who was edging along the stick toward his hand. I watched and then whooped with delight when Chou Chou suddenly pinched Athos's arm! Quickly, with his other hand, Athos grabbed the other end of the stick and let go his first grip, so that Chou Chou was far away from doing harm again with his strong bill. Gradually Chou Chou sidled toward the hand that was now holding the stick. At this point Athos thrust the stick into my hand! Chou Chou gave me a pinch and Athos, after all, had the last laugh.

Where were we to keep Chou Chou at night, so that in the morning before we were up he would not wreck the living room? We thought immediately of the shower rod in the bathroom, from which he could not get off until we took him. He protested vigorously at first, but soon learned patience with the people he had to put up with. Our friends protested that in *our* bathroom they had no privacy; I confess that going there at night and having macaw eyes staring at me was disconcerting, to say nothing of an impudent, insinuating voice saying "Hel-lo."

On fine days, we put the macaw outdoors in a dogwood tree at the entrance to the terrace in front of the house. He greeted each guest cordially, and he also knew how to say "good-bye," but, when being taught the parting word, his masters had often said, "Tell them good-bye," and Chou Chou had learned to use the whole phrase. On one memorable occasion our guests were delighted with Chou Chou, and when they were leaving we said, "Chou Chou, tell them good-bye." Promptly he said a polite good-bye. Fascinated by the bird, our guests lingered. Chou Chou cocked his head to one side and, in an emphatic, dictatorial voice, shouted: "TELL THEM GOOD-BYE!"

One day, while walking at the edge of a large field surrounded by thick trees and underbrush outside Fort Myers, Athos was attracted by the sound of raucous voices overhead. Two large green parrots! Had they been blown into Florida by a storm, as often happens with other non-native species across the Gulf of Mexico? They chased each other around the field, stopping at times in the treetops, and Athos watched them for half an hour before they disappeared in the trees.

While he was living near Fort Myers, outside his window was a mockingbird nest containing four young birds that he watched daily. Suddenly Athos was called to the window by alarm crying, then the noise of a crash which indicated that something was falling in the tree. For an instant he had a glimpse of a large bird, then it disappeared. He dashed out of the house and saw a beautiful swallow-tailed kite flying away, carrying something in his talons. Upon inspection of the mockingbird nest, Athos found that three of the fledglings were missing and the fourth was dead from a blow.

Mind you, Athos was not collecting memories

which later he would find useful in his work; he was simply enjoying himself, in the way he liked best. Contrasts in people's interests is something that fascinates me always. I remember the time on a train to St. Louis when Athos and I made a game of how many birds we could see from our windows, and we counted a remarkable number. Across the aisle were four men intent upon playing poker all day, and, so as not to be distracted by outside views, they carefully pulled down their window shades.

How many persons go to St. Louis on specific "bird business"? We were the guests of the St. Louis Bird Club, who determined that the Menabonis should have a memorable four days of every possible activity concerning birds to the last split second before leaving. One of the days we spent driving about St. Charles County, despite gasoline rationing, and saw birds of the Mississippi Flyway which we had heretofore seen rarely or not at all. To me there was a particular delight in learning the charming French names of two marshes, Marais Temps Clair and Marais Croche, which put me in the spirit of the early French settlers. I saw descendants of the birds of those pioneers: American egrets, shovellers, orchard orioles, herring gulls, house wrens (I realized that the species I saw for the first time had been everyday sights to those French people of olden days); the dickcissel, bronze grackle, king rail, cliff swallow, horned lark, black tern, yellow warbler, Baltimore oriole, and to climax the day, five blue geese.

Then, too, Athos and I have made innumerable visits to the different Golden Isles of Georgia. Our favorite was the privately owned Sapelo Island, and we got permission to visit Blackbeard Island, a U.S. wildlife refuge, separated by a river from Sapelo. Legend says that here pirate ships anchored in hiding. What would pirates have thought if they had known that someday their hideout would be considered treasure islands of birds? Athos and I could evoke no

Northern Oriole

enthusiasm over the possibility of pirate gold buried there, for we reveled in the wealth of birds.

As a side trip we once went to near-by Little Sapelo Island, to see an old rookery of wood ibis. It was deep in the heart of the smaller island at a natural pond whose soggy banks prevented our getting very close, and we were annoyed with ourselves for not having rubber boots. But we could easily see the crude tree nests, the trees streaked with white bird droppings, and the ground littered with molted white feathers. At the sight of us the two hundred large birds stood stiffly erect in alarm, or landed awkwardly on perches. When we came near they milled about in the air over their pond, making a striking picture of snowy whiteness.

On Sapelo proper, on the magnificent wide beach we found a piping plover who was paralyzed. The brown eyes held no fear of us, and he seemed to place his destiny in our hands. Alas, he died, but it was not from lack of attention, for we used all our human intelligence on that single bird. His destiny was to become a bird skin in a cabinet for an artist to study and to recapture in a measure his beauty and aliveness upon canvas.

We caught a boat-tailed grackle to enliven our Atlanta aviary. Frozen uncooked shrimp are plentiful in the markets now, but in those years I had such difficulty in finding them to feed our new pet that when I did have success I had difficulty in restraining myself from letting out loud whoops. (Indeed, this is only one of our many difficulties in securing the proper foods for our many birds.) Upon a subsequent visit to Sapelo, I commissioned an old Negro to make a shrimp hand-net for me, learned the technique of holding a portion of it between my teeth while I prepared to throw the net, and how to do so without yanking out my front teeth. When I saw dozens of wiggling shrimp in my catch, I was filled with glee. Better still was going out in a regular shrimp boat and watching the men drag their enormous net. I gloated over the thousands of shrimp that were hauled aboard. To this day every time I have shrimp to eat, I recall our pet boat-tailed grackle coming to get from our hands the shrimp I had such difficulty in buying for him in Atlanta.

We spent two weeks on Sapelo trying to trap a pair of adult-plumage painted buntings. These most exquisite of little birds are often called "nonpareil." There were hundreds of females and juveniles, greenish above and yellowish below, present on the lawn of our host, but we wanted one male with his various hues of blue, green, red, and purple. Athos had never painted them, and our host could not understand why he, with his special federal and state permits to shoot any kind of bird that was necessary for his work, did not help himself to a pair. But no, Athos wanted them alive, no matter the cost in effort. In vain we tried to lure one of the few adult males. Eventually he had to compromise by trapping three of the greenish birds in the hope that one of them, as it matured, would prove to be a male —which it did.

We have a photograph to prove that wild turkeys were so plentiful that often as we drove along woodland roads we had to stop the automobile to let a flock cross in front of us. Our hosts had a strawberry patch of which they were proud, and a mother turkey brought her eight poults every morning to help themselves to the luscious berries; there were plenty for all of us.

Once, while walking on the beach looking for sea-turtle eggs in the sand, we heard a commotion and saw something large on the shore but at quite a distance. Since we were thinking of turtles, we visualized a creature with flippers in motion. We had to walk a long way before getting close. Then we saw that it was a brown pelican, flapping his wings on the sand! Something was peculiar about his shape—Lord have mercy on his soul—the whole back of his body was missing!

As we got to the bird, he flapped his wings feebly for the last time. The sand was soaking up his drained lifeblood, and in front of his large pouch bill was dropped a freshly caught fish. To explain the tragedy we could only guess that, while diving into the water for the fish, a shark had bitten the pelican in two. Instinctively he had made his last desperate journey seeking safety, leaving a trail of blood.

One time I decided to keep a list of exactly what we saw on Sapelo Island, Georgia, between January 9 and 15, 1941. There was a flock of piping plovers, their yellowish nonwebbed feet running over the wet sand, then stopping abruptly as the birds pecked in the sand. A colony of semipalmated sandpipers. They were feeding at the edge of a pool of water left on the beach when the tide receded. They looked very busy dipping their bills into the water and sometimes immersing their entire heads. One took a splashing bath, two got into a fight, and then all took flight and, as they wheeled in the air, their white underparts glistened like silver. A herring gull was wary and kept just ahead of us on the beach for a mile or so. A Forster's tern passed over the water's edge, and in the background over the water flew several cormorants, occasionally relaxing to glide. And there I saw my first two oyster-catchers, with their conspicuous large red bills.

We sat on the edge of a dune with a sheer drop twenty-five feet to the tree line. There were cedars, longleaf pines, live oaks, and a mass of undergrowth and tangled vines. One lonely mourning dove flew out. Another day at this location we got our eastern ground dove, who was to be our house pet for many years.

I remember a certain day which was so vivid and bright that we had good visibility with or without field glasses. We were walking along the beach, which we had to ourselves, when Athos spied through the glasses a bird perching on a half-buried log. He announced that it was a burrowing owl. We started toward the bird, who could see us plainly and positively identify *us* as humans (or did we look like something else, all bundled as we were in several sweaters, mufflers, and gloves?). But when we were fifty feet from the log, the bird took flight. He went a hundred feet farther, before alighting on the beach to watch us, bobbing his head repeatedly. We examined the half-hollow palm log, finding much "bird sign": skeleton remains of past meals, and a great quantity of owl pellets disgorged after the digestion was complete. We remarked that the log must have been a favorite eating and sleeping place for the owl, since there was no good burrowing ground.

We went on toward the owl and this time got to within thirty feet of him before he again flew down the beach. This kept up all morning, as we ambled along the beach watching other bird life at the same time. After the burrowing owl reached the farthest point of the island, he flew inland to the trees to escape from us. For three successive days we saw this owl take off from the hollow log when we arrived at the beach.

Upon our return to Atlanta, I wrote of some of our Sapelo Island bird observations for the Georgia Ornithological Society publication, *The Oriole*, and mentioned the above about the burrowing owl. Later in the *Birds of Georgia, A Preliminary Check-list and Bibliography*, by Greene, Griffin, Odum, Stoddard, Tomkins, appeared: "Burrowing Owl; Speotyto cunicularia subsp. Mr. and Mrs. Athos Menaboni observed one on Sapelo Island on January 9, 1941. Absence of specimens from Georgia forces the species to remain on the Hypothetical List."

The point is that we did not shoot the burrowing owl to prove, by having a specimen, that we had seen it. At that time we had no idea that the burrowing owl had not been seen in Georgia before, but even if we had known, I do not believe that Athos would have shot the bird to prove it, despite the fact that he had his gun with him and is an expert marksman. To be sure, there must be rules set by scientists, or else persons who do not know much about birds can easily mistake one species for a similar one. Scientific facts must be correct beyond a shadow of doubt, which is why I write only of things we have witnessed ourselves.

Athos was thoroughly familiar with burrowing owls in Florida; in fact, once he had a unique and unexplainable experience. With some friends he was driving through the Kissimee Prairie when he saw at the side of the road and on a little elevation of ground a burrowing owl. He stopped

the car and the owl kept bobbing his head, apparently unconcerned. Athos walked to him, and the bird made no attempt to escape. Slowly Athos put his hand under him and the owl stepped onto the hand! Then Athos walked in the direction of the car to show the bird to his friends at close range, but when near the car, although not particularly frightened, the owl flew to another elevated spot. Athos was so surprised at what he had been able to do with the bird that he wondered if he could again pick him up. Once more he got the bird on his hand and carried him part way to the automobile before he flew away. Athos is still curious to know if the owl had been someone's escaped pet, although the bird was many miles from any habitation.

To refresh my memory of the experiences of the few days in January that I recorded in a notebook, I read the entire bird list. Perhaps, to anyone else, reading the list would become tiresome, but it is impressive to us that there were sixty-eight different names of birds on that list. I do not like to add long columns of figures, but to prove that Sapelo Island is a bird paradise I had better give the grand total of all the separate birds we saw: 4,523. Is it surprising that Athos and I loved that island?

The birds were everywhere, not only at the beach. As we walked inland from the shore we were under venerable live oaks, draped with gray beards of Spanish moss and, upon closer examination, a topping of curly ferns on each widespread limb. Beneath many limbs or on the sturdy trunk itself were round spots of whitish or gray-green or rosy lichens. I watched a squirrel scampering up a tree, bringing sudden life to the scene. At a safe distance he paused to scratch. Fleas? Ah, there was the flashing golden yellow of a meadow lark in flight; we heard crows cawing; and high above us a marsh hawk circled. In the distance we could hear pileated woodpeckers, and from a different direction the rolling call of a kingfisher. And on the same road another day

Painted Bunting

I made an entirely different list of birds that I saw there.

At the stableyard we could depend upon the same population day after day. In the lone moss-laden live oak tree were a tremendous number of male boat-tailed grackles, red-winged blackbirds, cowbirds, rusty blackbirds, and chattering and fighting English sparrows. We had never seen so many birds congregated in one tree. They would drop to the ground to feed in the trough with the horses and mules, walk on the ground near the hooves, then nonchalantly stroll over to a puddle of water to drink.

The fresh-water duck pond was an interesting place always. There were so many ducks that I really feel for any sportsman reading about them: pintails, mallards, black ducks, baldpates, ruddy ducks, ringnecks, scaups, shovellers, to say nothing of the coots and Florida gallinules that added to the crowd on the water's surface.

Once we saw four bald eagles flying over the pond at the same time. Another day we observed an eagle perched on a dead tree, watching an osprey catching a fish. Then we saw an exciting show: the eagle descended from his perch, headed straight for the osprey, harried him into dropping the newly caught fish, then dashed below, catching the fish in the air before it landed.

On a foggy morning at five, Athos visited this pond and secreted himself in a blind, armed only with camera and sketchbook. As dim light came he watched through the mist what seemed to be a large floating raft, and he thought it strange that he had never noticed a raft on the duck pond. It occurred to him that the wind was not blowing hard enough to make the dark raft move so rapidly toward him. When it was ten feet away, he realized that what he was seeing was a compact body of lesser scaups, undoubtedly assembled in this manner for self-protection during the night. He estimated that there were at least five hundred birds.

While he was observing a second raft of these scaups, there was a sudden confusion and noisy diving in every direction. A great shadow descended from the sky in the midst of the diving scaups, striking right and left. Before Athos could recover from his surprise, it disappeared. A bald eagle—which left empty-handed.

The same morning he saw a thousand or more coots, literally covering the pond. Athos was so intent upon his observations that he forgot to use his camera or sketchbook; he was too busy storing in his memory the wealth of birds that were collected on that Golden Isle.

That morning I had not been an early riser, but had stayed abed while Athos went afield to see his birds. I might just as well have remained in my bed in Atlanta. Fortunately Sapelo Island was fabulously wealthy in birds and I could squander them, knowing that there were plenty more thousands waiting for me.

There are so many interesting things to collect pertaining to birds that we know we have made a mere beginning, and wonderful days lie ahead of us. For instance, this morning I feel impelled to start collecting bird legends. Athos has come into the house to tell me about the Negroes, Ike, Byrd, and a new man, "Snow," who, while at their work, were talking about the eagle carrying away human babies. It is an old folk story that they believe in spite of Athos's telling them that science has disproved the legend.

Athos had moved a little distance from them, and overheard Snow tell the following: "Very few folks know that the eagle has a precious stone in its head. It's a diamond and not many folks can find it but it's there. This is why not many folks can kill eagles. The diamond is worth a million hundred dollars."

CHAPTER SIX

I LIKE STORIES, either fiction or true; it does not matter which, so long as I have them. When I want a true nature story, all I have to do is to ask Athos for one from his past.

I have always been grateful to the female English sparrow that Athos had bought in a little wooden cage for ten centimes when he was a small boy. When Athos was punished for not studying his school lessons by having all his birds freed, this sparrow came home at dusk to her boy-master to keep his heart from being entirely broken.

From that day on, she flew in and out the open window as she chose. Each noon when Athos came from school, she would at his whistle fly down from the trees on the boulevard, perch on his shoulder, and come into the house with him for lunch. In the dining room she would fly around the table and, should she not be offered enough to eat, she would land on his shoulder to peck his ear lobe until he fed her amply. She knew that she belonged to Athos and that he belonged to her.

The first mating season, Athos wondered if she would desert him; however, she fought off all ardent males. Only once through the years did she make a nest and lay eggs, and they were infertile. For eleven years she was Athos's favorite pet but one day when Athos was not at home she flew indoors. His mother took the visibly sick bird in her hand, and there, of old age, she died.

After hearing Athos's story of this sparrow, I began to wish for a little sparrow in my life. When I was a young girl my favorite Sunday-

school song ended: "For His eye is on the sparrow, and I know He watches me." Those words had moved me tremendously; if God watched over a sparrow, He was watching me also.

One day my telephone rang, and one of the little girls from a school where I had given a bird talk told me that she had a baby bird for me to raise, which she thought was a towhee. When I went to get it, I found that at long last I had a sparrow for my very own, just as Athos had had long ago. I gave my sparrow the name of Charlotte, after the girl who had given it to me, in the hope that it would prove to be a female and the name would be fitting. It did fit! Athos's childhood bird had been a female and mine was the same.

I promised to tell you about Charlotte. Here's her story:

Charlotte had a strong maternal instinct while still a baby herself. We fed her by hand and with a mouthful of food she went straight to the vireo twins she had adopted. Vireos were supposed to have a diet different from that of a sparrow and, fearing that the vireos would sicken from Charlotte's feeding, we shut them in a cage to prevent her from getting to them. Charlotte was frantic and, with her little wings fluttering madly against the bars, she fought to get to her babies. The twins cried pitifully for her and came to the bars for their feeding. After we watched this unhappy struggle, we decided to let nature take its course and allow them to do as they wished. What a happy reunion! As the vireos were insect-eating birds, we gave them supplementary feeding. Insect-eating fledglings are hard to raise indoors; certainly it was not through neglect by Charlotte that the vireos died in a few weeks. I detected that Charlotte missed them the first day, but after that her interests became allied with the blue jay and flicker fledglings that we had at the same time, although she made no attempts to mother them.

In time she chose her own sleeping place, on a shelf by the fireplace behind an antique coffeepot. She belligerently protected herself from intrusion by other birds at night and would not even let an indigo bunting perch on a shelf above hers. As she turned to face the wall, she had no idea that we and our visitors could see her rear at one side of the coffeepot. Of all the objects of art upon the ten shelves by the fireplace, Charlotte got the most attention, or rather, her tail did.

Charlotte had nice table manners. At breakfast she learned to wait until our cereal was fixed, at which time she could alight on the side of a bowl to help herself to corn flakes and drink the sweetened milk. Sometimes she sat still on the table until her sweetened coffee was given to her in a spoon. At other meals she found that as long as she did not get on our plates and remained standing on the table, she could eat from the side of the plate whatever she wished. It might be bits of chicken or pie pastry or anything else she wanted. She was very neat and clean; after she had finished her meal, in lieu of a napkin, she flew to our shoulders to wipe off her bill on our collars!

She learned that she could get outdoors after breakfast by flying against the glass door to indicate to us that she wanted it opened. She would frolic outdoors all day, returning at twilight to the door to be let inside. When she wanted that door opened she meant that very instant! Should we be going out somewhere before dark, a whistle would bring her inside any time of the afternoon. Our friends were delighted to see us open the door, and whistle a certain tune. From nowhere—whish—there was Charlotte turning a corner and darting inside the house making a landing on the lamp. If it was near her bedtime, she helped herself to the seeds of the ground dove, took a sip of water, and went directly to her shelf to sleep.

Charlotte was content to go no farther from the house than a hundred feet or so. Whenever she was hungry she found provisions on the feeding station. At our lunch- or teatime she peered in the window by the dining table, and if she saw some food that she wanted she flew to the door to be let inside to share our meal. She liked us to eat at the belvedere or have company refreshments there, for Charlotte enjoyed joining us outdoors for her portion of good things to eat; anyone could hold out a cracker to her and she would eat it on the outstretched hand.

Either outdoors or indoors, when I sat down, Charlotte came to give me a "manicure," that is, bite my fingernails. Often she would come flying to my shoulder and when I turned my head toward her, she gave me a kiss on my mouth. The imp sometimes bit my lips and I'd slap her. I swear that she laughed in my face! To make up, she would snuggle on my neck affectionately, and what could I do but forgive the little devil? Then she'd decide that the short hairs on my neck needed to be plucked and she'd give a yank, and I'd let out a yell and chase her away.

On rainy or cold days she preferred to stay in the house. There were plenty of things to do inside, such as tease Zulu, for she found the marmoset tail hairs fascinating to pull; or fight the indigo bunting, who was bullied by her; or annoy the ground dove while she was feeding. Of all the attractions in the house, she liked the grosbeak in his cage best of all, and for hours she would sit on top of the cage just looking at him, although he paid no attention whatsoever.

A year passed and the mating season arrived. No English sparrows came to our sanctuary and Charlotte did not know that she, a country lass, would have to go to town to find a husband. She flew about with straw in her bill trying to show someone that she was interested in setting up housekeeping, but no sparrows came around.

At this time, in the house she became exasperatingly mean and spiteful with the indigo

Red-winged Blackbird

bunting, although, goodness knows, he never once cast an amorous glance at her to provoke her wrath and did his best to keep out of her way. Charlotte began wooing the grosbeak with all her feminine wiles. He ignored her, which did not dampen her enthusiasm for cavorting and trying to entice him. To see what would happen, we let the grosbeak out of his cage for several days. Charlotte was shameless and did her utmost to lure him, but he was simply not interested. When he was again put in his cage, she knew there was no use hoping that he might become her mate; however, she felt platonic affection toward him despite his indifference, and enjoyed being close to him atop his cage.

There was another summer of flitting in and out of the house and having fun at all times. She was now over a year old and occasionally she spent the night out—just to be devilish.

When, late in August, she spent a night out, we thought nothing of it, nor of the fact that she did not come in the house the next day, for we saw her outdoors and knew she could find enough to eat on the feeding station. However, that evening she came inside with puffed feathers and lackluster eyes, and we were concerned to see her sick. We were thankful that she wanted to eat supper, for many ill birds refuse food. Possibly it was a minor indisposition. The next morning she ate some breakfast, but we could see that she was sicker. She did not want to go outdoors; all she wanted to do was to sit near her beloved grosbeak. Had she eaten something outdoors that had disagreed with her, or had she contracted some disease?

The following day she showed signs of something being wrong with her feet, for she could not land properly after flight, but toppled over. She abandoned her shelf sleeping place and stayed on top of the grosbeak cage, having difficulty perching there. The next morning, to our dismay, we found that her legs and feet were partially paralyzed, her flight uncontrolled and erratic.

Ten days after she first became ill, Charlotte was paralyzed all over, with the exception of her eyes, which were normal, and her bill, which she could open part way. I had never felt so sorry for any creature. She lay prone in a box, not even able to move her neck. Charlotte, who had been so gay, carefree, and active, now lay utterly helpless. Her one comfort was to be close to her grosbeak. He gave her no attention, but that did not matter to Charlotte, she just wanted to look at him.

She was entirely dependent upon us. Whenever she wanted anything to eat or drink, she called to us with a pitiful cry. We had to put soft food at the tip of her bill, and, so that she could drink, dip her bill into water. We put cod-liver oil in her food, and we placed her in the sun so that the beneficial rays might help heal her. We covered Charlotte at night to keep her warm, and in the morning when she heard us moving about she called to us to come take her out of bed.

We coddled her and talked to her and, in response to our display of affection, she gave a contented little chatter-chatter. When I sat down to read for hours aloud I held Charlotte in my cupped hands, and every so often she would peep-peep softly to let me know that she liked being in my hands.

Did she have polio? Every day, every hour we flexed her legs and wings, to try to keep her muscles from hardening and to make her blood circulate. Someone told our doctor of having recently seen a paralyzed sparrow, and not long afterwards one with crippled feet came to his own feeding station. Athos and a friend found an adult male English sparrow in a city gutter as paralyzed as our Charlotte, and Athos brought him home; but the newcomer, an old bird not accustomed to ministering by people, would not eat and was so frightened that he died in a couple of days. Was there an epidemic of paralysis of sparrows in Atlanta? If so, how did Charlotte

contract her disease, since we had never had English sparrows at our sanctuary from whom she could catch it? How was the germ carried?

As I held our sick bird in my hands, I knew how Athos's mother had felt long years ago when that sick sparrow in Italy came to her and died. Would Charlotte die? She was too young! I remembered my own mother singing with me, "For His eye is on the sparrow, and I know He watches me."

There was nothing that we, mere mortals, could do except give her all the affection she craved and attend to her bodily needs. She could wiggle a bit, and often got into awkward positions from which we had to extricate her; unless we kept her propped up with wadded cloth she lay on her breast, which became bare from the friction wearing off the feathers. New feathers came all over her, encased in their sheathing, and she looked much like a porcupine. Since she could do no preening, we brushed and cleaned her as best we could, but those new feather sheaths were a problem for us. When she got dirty we dipped her in warm water and put her in the sun to dry, for she could not shake away the wetness, nor could we dry her with a towel except partially. Poor Charlotte was in a bad way; would she be an invalid thus for years?

As the weeks passed, several people seeing Charlotte in such a pitiful plight said that we should put her out of her misery. Kill Charlotte, when she looked to us for her salvation? We continued to watch over her with all the tender care we would have given a sick person.

More weeks passed. While there was life in her there was hope.

Then one day she stood up! She wobbled and fell down, but that was all right as a first attempt. I admit that I was so happy that I cried.

How we encouraged her to try—try—try. The next day she actually took three steps before tumbling over. Daily she improved in walking, and began fluttering her wings feebly. After a few days of wing exercises, she took her first flight. True, it was queer and drunken flying and she landed on her head, but we told her not to mind, and she picked herself up and tried again. We complimented her and made such a fuss over her courageous attempts that I believe she tried for our sakes. Charlotte was no longer a helpless invalid!

Now, December 10, Charlotte is quite her old self, as though nothing had happened to her, except that she does not yet want to go outdoors. Fortunately, she does not have to battle the elements and fight for a livelihood, but can continue to stay in her very own home with the people who love her.

Again she is gay and blithe, and so are we. A few minutes ago I saw her teasing Zulu on the hearth, deviling the life out of him until he had to speak crossly to her. She understood and changed her attitude toward him. Now she is snuggling close to the marmoset, not for the warmth of his furry body, for she could have got as much heat elsewhere on the hearth, but to display affection toward him.

I know what John Burroughs meant when he said, "I go to books and to nature as a bee goes to a flower, for a nectar that I can make into my own honey." The trouble I have, though, is that I get the two all mixed up, never quite sure whether I am living fiction or reality, and what the product will be after it is distilled.

In literature I constantly run across such phrases as "the cricket on the hearth" and the "dove of peace"—symbolic expressions—yet *I* had to make them into the real thing. First I had to get a hearth, and, after I did, the living cricket moved in on it! You'd think I would be content with that symbol an actuality, but no, I had to have that "dove of peace" too. Give me enough time and I will make fiction into a true story: I have a dove on my hearth! There has never been a fireplace ornament to equal her. There is something indefinably cozy and peaceful about a wood fire anyway, but to see a minute dove sitting on the hearth adds the finishing touch.

The eastern ground dove is the smallest of wild pigeons; our little lady is about six and a half inches in length, including her tail. Her head and neck are small in proportion to the rest of her plump body. She has orange-red eyes; her bill is coral-red; her feet and legs are daintily flesh-colored; indeed, her whole appearance is sleekly well groomed and delicate, making feminine visitors exclaim, "She is adorable. So that is what the true dove colors are!" Her wee size makes her very endearing and I have seen grown men grow really sentimental over her.

People may look at her, but she resents being touched. She has one wing only, and, when anyone stoops to the floor to pet her, she tries to fly away and always tumbles. At such a moment one can catch a glimpse of the conspicuous terracotta red under her wing. She gets provoked and irritated at such moments, and the more hasty and nervous she is the more somersaults she turns. Regaining some degree of calm finally, she manages to keep an upright position and

pigeon-toed and with mincing steps she walks hastily away. As she goes, her head bobs back and forth and her tail is raised. Her feelings are hurt and she sits in her corner sulking until Athos "talks" in her language.

I cannot imitate her, but Athos can. The two have duets, or rather, ask each other repeatedly, "Who-who-oo?" At any time Athos wishes he can call her to come sit contentedly for hours at his feet. When she is annoyed or wants to warn us or Yama that we are about to step on her she has a different tone of voice, a whining "woo-oo-oo!" Her calls are deceptive, sounding as though they came from far away, and we have to be on the lookout for her and careful where we step.

She walks a great deal, appearing to have a definite objective in getting somewhere fast. Anyone who liked a spotlessly clean house would not like to see the dove on her floor feeding tray scattering her seeds far and wide; however, she is a big help to me in picking up crumbs under the dining-room table. One spring she laid two tiny white eggs on the rug. We felt badly that they were not fertile. But there was no point in

the eggs being entirely wasted—each was the proper size for a marmoset meal—and Zulu liked them very much.

In warm weather she takes daily splashing baths in the water bowl provided for her and keeps immaculately clean. Also she likes to take sun baths, follows the sunshine from window to window, and raises her wing high to let the sun rays get beneath it.

During the five winters we have had her, she has spent much of her time on the hearth. She gets as close to the open fire or the hot ashes as she dares, often causing us fear for her safety. One of the things our friends like to see is the way she backs up to the fire, lifts her tail and warms her rump.

I cannot grasp her in my hand, just as the ultimate in peace cannot be grasped, but I can get very close to my dove. Our "dove of peace" is not a mere word symbol or picture of a bird flying in the air with an olive branch in her bill; she is living in our house.

While reading together, we often stop to have a discussion of what we have read, picking out points that are of particular significance to our personal lives. Sometimes we disagree as to what moral the author intended to convey and have fun arguing about it. Many an author would be surprised to learn what has impressed us most.

This morning I have looked out my window to see some beautiful birds in our aviary, and have recalled the joys we have experienced through the possession of them. Throngs of visitors have seen these birds here, and I have wondered if they have been curious to know the story of how we got them and to what trouble we have gone to secure models for the paintings. Certainly William Beebe should be amused, for his book *Pheasants: Their Lives and Homes* started the story.

We had almost finished reading Dr. Beebe's book when a long-distance telephone call came from a man who asked if either Athos or I would dash up to New York to discuss a matter of business with him. At the moment Athos could not go, so I entered into the spirit of going on a lark. One thing was uppermost in Athos's mind: "In Atlanta we have not been able to find a pair of ring-necked pheasants, but New Jersey has many pheasantries. Do not come back until you have got a pair for me." As I departed, his command was repeated.

Frightened of New York, I asked my sister-in-law, Tommy, to come from Jersey into the city with me. We arrived an hour before our appointment, which Tommy said was to the good for, before transacting any business, we had to buy new hats. We purchased them—mine was covered with pink roses—and then were prepared as women must be.

The business matter attended to satisfactorily, I went home with Tommy to New Jersey for a little visit, bearing in mind my other piece of business—the securing of a pair of live pheasants for Athos. Talk about detective sleuthing, we ran up quite a telephone bill with toll calls about the state, on the trail of pheasants. We were told that

many of the game farms had closed during the war, and I began to be fearful that I could not secure the birds for Athos. But if he wanted a pair of ring-necked pheasants, then it was my job to get them.

Eventually we learned about a certain pheasantry that did not have a telephone and, with our new hats on and despite gasoline rationing, Tommy and I drove many miles into the country. When I saw thousands of penned pheasants, I could scarcely contain myself for joy.

Nope, the man said, he could not sell me a pair of birds, for he had already sold the entire lot to the state of New Jersey, to be released for hunting purposes. We said that one pair would not be missed, that one pair was needed by an artist—but no, the man was firm. I cocked my rose-covered hat to a more becoming angle on my head and went to work. Tommy and I were invited into the kitchen to have coffee with the man and his wife. I attribute it to my hat with pink roses that I finally broke down his resistance. But nope, he would not ship the two birds, nor would he crate the pheasants for me to express; he would put them into a burlap bag, "and take 'em or leave 'em." I took them!

The problem then was how to get them to Atlanta. After much thought we settled on the idea of putting the pheasants in a dog's traveling case. I knew that pheasants in captivity when frightened have the habit of jumping up, sometimes batting out their brains, so we padded the inside of the top of the traveling case.

My next problem was getting home myself. It was then two o'clock, and by telephone we learned that the streamline train was leaving New York at four-thirty, but there was no hope of my getting on it, since I did not have a reservation. However, perhaps I could get on the ten-o'clock train that night. I said that I would get on the four-thirty train.

At Penn Station we found a lady whose job it was to help people out of jams. There was no

cancellation of a reservation, but the lady took us to the gate to see the uniformed man who comes up from the train, to see if he could help us at the last moment after everyone had gone through the gate. She explained to the man and at the last moment he told me to hop on another train that was leaving also for Washington, and when there to see him again and he would give me a seat to Atlanta. Quickly I said, "Remember I have on a hat with pink roses," and I ran to the other gate to board the Washington train.

In Washington, where no redcaps were in sight and the platforms were endless miles, I had to run like mad, carrying my suitcase and those pheasants, who weighed a ton or two. Breathless and weary, I found the right gate for the stream-line train, where there were others who were hoping to get on at the last minute. I *had* to get on, for, as it was, my two birds were undergoing the cruelty of doing without food or water for seventeen hours.

I spied the uniformed trainman coming and, in my loud voice, I called to him: "Remember me—the hat with the pink roses! In New York you promised to give me a seat here." He smiled, scribbled something on a piece of paper, and I scrambled through the gate, to race more miles along a platform with my heavy burdens.

I found the right car, the right seat number —next to a girl. I moved aside a folded newspaper and sank down exhausted. She said, "That seat belongs to someone else."

"A man or a woman?"

"A man. He has stepped out a moment."

"Thank goodness." I continued to sit.

After the train started, the man returned to his seat, and we compared our slips of paper, both identical. Politely he told me to stay where I was until the conductor came through, when I, who had got on last, would be assigned another seat. After a while the conductor, and my friend in uniform, came and assigned me to another car. The nice man, who was getting back his original seat, offered to carry my luggage to the other seat.

On the entire trip there was not a peep out of my pheasants and no one knew what was in the traveling case. If they jumped up against the padding, I never knew it. In fact, their long tails did not even get broken.

There had been no time to send Athos a telegram as to when I was arriving in Atlanta and to meet me in the automobile. At the station I telephoned home, but there was no answer; and I remembered that it was his day off from painting and that he would be outdoors far from where he could hear the telephone bell. I lugged my cases to a bus and went to the nearest place of public transportation to our house in the country. I telephoned again and got no answer. I had spent all my money, did not have my checkbook with me, and did not have taxi fare.

I telephoned to my neighbor, who said that his wife was in her car shopping near me, and to look for her in one of the stores she and I frequented. I went out onto the street—to step right into her automobile! She told me that she had seen the pretty hat with pink roses, wondered who wore it—and then saw it was me.

I got out of the car to open my gate, spotted Athos a hundred feet distant in our woods, and called to him; it was the first he knew that I was within a thousand miles of him. He was glad that I had come home, for he does not know how to cook anything except fried eggs and he was sick of the sight of them.

I was about to tell the details of my trip, when Athos noticed the traveling case, which was new to him, and asked what was in it. I told him.

He was so beside himself with joy at having the new birds that I had no opportunity to tell of my experiences. Those pheasants got all the attention.

In the house alone (for Athos was enjoying the pheasants in the aviary) I put on my apron to start cooking lunch. Then I remembered that I still had on my rose-covered hat. I took it off and had a laugh that it had cost me only a dollar ninety-eight!

And so this bird artist secures his models to pose for him. I do not know how writers ever get their books finished. This minute Athos is plaguing me to come see at close range the female Cooper's hawk perching atop his worktable. "Isn't she beautiful? Isn't she wonderful?" As he scratches the back of her head, he continues talking, "Who says that Cooper's hawks can't be tamed?"

CHAPTER SEVEN

*I*T IS DECEMBER 13, and the thermometer reads 30°. Slow rain is freezing into long icicles, and the icy weight is bending the pine trees. It gives me the shivers to look outside, but why need I look outside, when on my desk is an exquisite white camellia brought to me last night by an out-of-town couple I had never met before? And why not look within me? It is the perfect day to think about flowers.

The highlight of every spring during my childhood was my father's announcement to my sister and me that it was time to hunt for trailing arbutus. Out came the botany book for Louise and me to read in case we had forgotten how the trailing plant with its small pale-pink flowers looked.

With keen anticipation we were off to search the hills about Rome for the flowers. We climbed, puffing and straining, clambering over jutting boulders, on narrow paths along high precipices, helping each other when the going was difficult. Although I was unaware of it at the time, father often must have been frightened to see his children in dangerous places. Perhaps that was part of the training he desired for us. My sister and I actually squealed over the fun of getting skinned knees and bramble-scratched legs, for that was part of adventuring.

Waiting for us to be smart enough to locate them and somewhere on the most inaccessible part of a mountainside were the tiny, sweetly perfumed, delicately colored flowers lying hidden under dead leaves. We were keyed to so high a pitch of excitement that tiredness, sore muscles, and torn dresses were nothing. If we had come too

early in the season, we did not return home with the feeling of defeat, for we could expect triumph the following Sunday. And we hung on every word father said as he explained the mysteries of nature. On those occasions he always quoted "The Flower in the Crannied Wall," and we felt that someday he would explain to us the greatest mystery of all, the impulse that started all creation.

Up, up we climbed, stopping often to poke amid the fallen leaves. Suddenly there would be a shout: "I've found it!" Then everyone would hasten to see, smell, and exclaim over the flowers. Father told us to pick only a few flowers, for we must leave the plants to grow more for us the next year. Proudly we returned home, having the added pleasure of telling mother about our success.

I wonder how many fathers take their children to hunt these flowers today—indeed, how many persons have seen an arbutus? Although I have climbed the Alps searching for edelweiss, I do not remember it as being as much fun as my earlier experiences in the Georgia hills seeking the trailing arbutus.

Fortunately, the love of flowers was instilled in me early in life. After Athos started painting bird pictures, we recognized that it was of prime importance to learn about flora as well as avifauna, for the plants were an integral part of each picture. Take, for instance, the pine; he had to paint the right-textured bark for each species, the exact length of the needles, and the proper number of needles in a bundle on a branch. If the artist did not paint the pine accurately, a tree expert could point out a fault, just as an ornithologist would notice if one feather on a bird was missing.

While we lived in the apartment, our friends helped supply the needed flora for the bird pictures. From Highlands, North Carolina, one friend brought carloads of mountain laurel, rhododendron, white pine, galax leaves, partridge berries, and other plants that would survive the trip to Atlanta. Another brought to us such flowers as pink moccasin flower, yellow lady's-slipper, white trillium—plants that had to be painted immediately before they wilted. All our friends, in securing plants for Athos to paint, found a new interest in the outdoors.

Not only our personal friends wanted to be helpful. Let me give some instances of how nice strangers have been.

One day Athos needed magnolia grandiflora for a picture, and I started out in the automobile not knowing where I could find a magnolia tree. After driving some time, I spotted such a tree in a yard. I approached a boy playing on the steps, and in reply to my question of whether or not his mother was at home he said, "My grandmother is. I'll get her."

I introduced myself to the lady. She had never heard the name, nor anything about the pictures, but after I told her what I desired, she said, "I'll be glad to give you all you want. Go select the prettiest magnolia blossoms while I get clippers to cut them."

I located a curving branch with two blossoms and a bud that I thought Athos would like for the composition of his picture. The lady insisted that I take home more than that one branch, and gave me great armfuls of magnolias. She went further than that: she insisted that whenever Athos needed magnolias for other pictures I was to come straight to her for all I wanted. Need I add that she became a good friend?

Then there was the time Athos needed some Cherokee roses and, although it was the state flower, nowhere could I locate a specimen. However, everyone I approached suggested where I could try further. Day after day I hunted—almost despairing—but if Athos needed the Cherokee rose it was my job to find it.

A nurseryman told me to telephone a certain lady who might have Cherokee roses. I telephoned to her, stated my business, and she interrupted a sentence by saying, "Why, Mrs. Menaboni, I've wanted to know you for years! Come to my house right now and if my rose is the Cherokee, you are welcome to have it." Her rose was not the Cherokee, but again I found a new friend.

But what of the Cherokee roses for Athos? Casually I happened to mention my vain search to a close friend. She laughingly said, "Sara, let this be a lesson to you. You should have come to me in the first place, for I have Cherokee roses all over one wall. Haven't you and Athos ever noticed them?"

To carry the Cherokee rose subject even further, the past summer I told an out-of-town friend about my experience in locating this rose for Athos to paint. When she returned to Hartsfield, South Carolina, she sent us eight Cherokee roses to plant. That settled that!

When we moved to the rented country home, it was interesting to learn for ourselves the difference between jack-in-the-pulpit and dragonroot; hairy Solomon's-seal and false Solomon's-seal; to find our first showy orchis; to discover the lizard's-tails in the brook, wild geranium, pasture rose, Indian pipe, all the violets and asters—but need I name every flower we learned to identify and enjoy?

Friends and flowers, I like to dwell upon them as Christmastime approaches. There comes to mind an incident that occurred the year after World War II started in Europe. Although letters went through to Italy, no more packages could be sent, and Athos was miserable at not being able to send a Christmas gift to his mother. Then he remembered: friends and flowers. Posthaste he dispatched a letter to Livorno to a lifelong friend. He enclosed a card.

That Christmas Day a delivery boy knocked at his mother's door. She was given a huge bouquet of fragrant violets, with the card attached reading, "To Mama, with love from Athos."

We found out later that Athos's friend on his

own initiative had gone a step further, nor had he taken credit for his act. The bouquet of violets with the card from Athos was tied with ribbon to a bottle of champagne.

This December 15 everything is covered with sleet and snow-powder. After breakfast I went outdoors with my camera, while Athos was busy with some pine saplings that the ice storm had uprooted. Pines come a dime a dozen here, so why was he tying them with wire to anchors, using rubber guards on their trunks to prevent bites into the bark, and tamping the icy soil firmly? What made him work so hard on those small pines? There is a reason for everything, of course.

Perhaps my husband remembers a certain day while we were living at the rented country home. I had been filled with feelings of frustration, self-pity, and depression that day and had written in my notebook: "A crow passes overhead, cawing raucously, and were I a bird I would scream in the same voice." I was silent, but I wrote down my turbulent thoughts that day long ago when I went for a last look at the beautiful woods that I loved.

There were many hardwood and other deciduous trees, wild flowers, and bushes, but those woods were notable for the tremendous pines. Not scrubby, spindly pines of recent growth, but majestic trees that had seen generations of people come and go. They were handsome trees that had been spared the ax and left as a legacy for future generations. I was the last person to see them standing in their glory—see them with appreciative eyes as masterpieces in nature.

I stood still, in order to concentrate upon what was mine at the moment but would not be mine after that day. The hot June sun brought out the odor of the pine needles. I wondered how many curious eyes were focused upon me, how many creatures were ready for instant flight should I move. I was immobile, wanting the creatures to

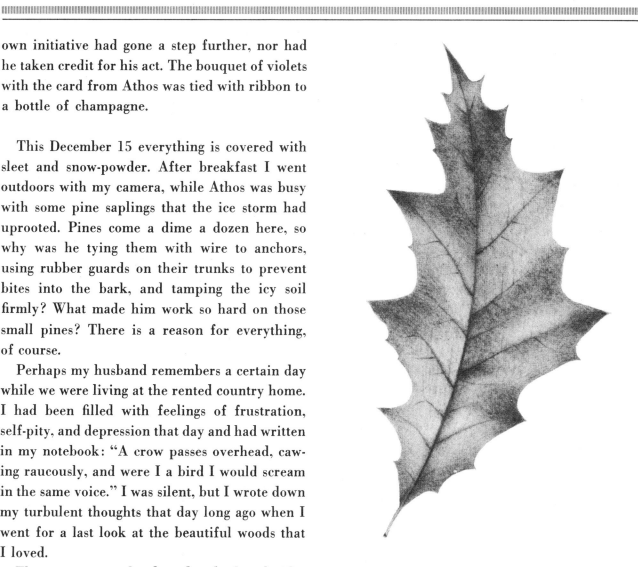

have their lovely moment also, for too soon there would be fearful scurrying under the fragrant pines.

A hooded warbler obligingly came to rest in a tree ten feet away and sang out his heart for me. I enjoyed his song the more because he had no cause to be afraid of me. He spied an insect, streaked off for the chase, and made a half turn in the air as he succeeded in catching it. He hurried away, perhaps to feed some hungry waiting mouth.

Then I sat on the brown pine needles beside a great trunk whose size shrank my ego. At the base grew a cluster of wild ginger, and two fronds of uncurling fern. I noticed charred evidences of a long-ago forest fire that the tree had withstood. In the crannies of the rough bark were lichen that gave the trunk a mellowed, venerable appearance. I felt even more dwarfed as I looked up. The tree had climbed into the air toward the sun, halting only for the seasons. I leaned against the tree, and touched the past. Long before I was born, wind had swayed the branches, raindrops had glistened countless times at the ends of the countless needles, and yellow dustlike pollen had covered the ground with a layer of gold—how many times? Some of the branches had been twisted by tussles with storms into fantastic shapes that would have been the joy of Oriental artists. The dark green of the needles made the woods magnificent in winter when all other trees had lost their foliage; and when new shoots came the trees resembled old-fashioned Christmas trees lit with candles. Instead of decorations of tin and glass, there had been red birds and blue birds and yellow birds.

While I looked up, a crested flycatcher came to perch on the lowest branch, sixty or seventy feet high. From a near-by and lower tree came the bell tones of a wood thrush. My eye was caught by a red-headed woodpecker walking up the trunk of a pine, then stopping to prop his spiny-tipped tail against the bark to rest. Under some bushes I could hear the henlike scratching sounds of a towhee or two among the leaves on the ground. These beautiful woods had been the haunt of innumerable generations of birds who had owned the trees, the bushes, the ground.

An airplane droned overhead, and I saw the yellow plane gleaming in the sun, to remind me of the man-made world from which I had escaped briefly: Far away a war was in progress. Progress!

That morning I had learned from the owner of the land that the pines were to be cut. Athos and I had tried to dissuade the owner from ruining the woods, to no avail; ready cash was desired and the trees would provide it. As I looked at the august trees my soul rebelled against my inability to do anything to prevent this ruin. The thought of money nauseated me as I looked at the trees that were not mine to keep intact.

I heard the woodcutters arrive. So soon? I took one last look, then sick at heart I fled to the house.

A short time later I heard one tree crash with a rending noise that made me wince involuntarily with pain. It was as though I personally were being injured. I heard another—and another—and, as the trees fell, my spirits went down and down.

I did not go into the mutilated woods again. Yet in the days that followed I could not avoid seeing the yellow of a stump that stood out boldly amid the greens and browns of the landscape, or the tops and lopped-off pine branches cluttering the ground where I remembered there had been pink and orange azaleas and sweet shrubs. There was a huge gash in the side of an old oak trunk where a falling pine had wrenched off a limb. One side was sheared off what had once been a perfectly shaped beech. The irreparable damage to other trees, caused by the falling pines, had been of no concern to the unsupervised woodcutters, for they had been interested only in getting out the lumber as quickly as possible. After the workmen had finished cutting and hauling, a last load must not have been worth returning to get, for they left one huge pine lying on the ground. Ah, well, pine borers would enjoy feasts.

From my window now at Valle Ombrosa I see a dozen or more great pines. One, a grandfather, is so close to our house that people have voiced the fear that a storm might cause it to fall on the house, and have given their emphatic opinion that it should be cut. The tree is ours. It remains. I see a white-breasted nuthatch walking head-down upon the trunk.

A heavy snow is falling this December morning. As we watched the birds at the feeding

Bufflehead

station outside our window, we were glad that we had put a roof over the station for just such a weather condition as this. At the station was a cafeteria line-up of a hermit thrush, a chipping sparrow, slate-colored juncoes, Carolina black-capped chickadees, tufted titmice, white-breasted nuthatches, Carolina wrens, red-eyed towhees, white-throated sparrows, goldfinches, and, most beautiful of all against the background of snow, five male cardinals.

Athos surveyed the landscape from the window and exclaimed, "All this snow is ours! No one can touch it or our birds."

At the moment I am grateful to the snow for giving me an excuse not to hustle into the city for Christmas shopping. Yesterday I was pondering over what to give Athos that would be extra-special, and was watching the mallards and Canada geese swimming on the lake, when nature gave me the answer to my problem. All I had to do was to write a letter enclosing a check.

I did not tell Athos what his surprise would be on Christmas, although he was curious and asked many questions. "Will I like it?" I told him that he would like it better than anything else I could buy for him. "How do you know positively that I will think it is beautiful?" I guaranteed that he would be pleased with the beauty of it. "Will it be the right size?" The gift would be the perfect size.

All the while he was questioning me I was chuckling inside, for it was funny that he did not guess what the present would be—for he was at that moment painting a picture of wood ducks! A pair of living wood ducks swimming on the lake will be the finishing touch to his lake project.

There is a still more significant aspect to this gift, and I should give the background for it.

I go back to the time we moved to the rented country home and ordered a pair of wood ducks from California. When they arrived, Athos was speechless over the small tree ducks that were so

brilliantly colored and intricately marked. He said that an artist, using all his imagination, could not dream up anything more gorgeous. It was true. They had such riotous colors that they seemed unreal; they might have been carved wooden ducks painted by an Oriental artist; but when the drake squeaked in his odd high-pitched little voice, and they decided to bathe in the sunken bathtub, then I knew they were very much alive.

They made themselves at home in one of the aviaries, and I felt about those wood ducks as a mother must feel who tries not to show partiality toward a cherubic baby, when there are other beloved children less angelic-looking. Yet it is natural to be swayed emotionally by exceptional beauty.

Athos spent much of his time at the two aviaries that had been sturdily constructed, and worked arduously to make everything ideal for the birds—as ideal as living on rented property allowed. He studied the myriad birds, he painted them, but best of all he enjoyed them to the utmost. Although we no longer had the woods that had been mutilated, at least we had our birds.

Then came a night when the wind howled, thunder rolled, and rain beat the earth. At dawn all was calm and serene. Suddenly, Athos sat upright in bed with a jerk that awakened me. With alarm in his voice he exclaimed, "I do not hear the morning calls of the birds!"

He scrambled into his clothes and rushed outdoors.

Something was drastically wrong. I got up to face the crisis that I knew subconsciously was coming.

Athos returned to the house a very sick man. During the night's storm, when we could not hear the distress calls from the largest aviary, dogs, leaving their telltale tracks in the mud, had broken through the wire to kill many of our birds. Evidently they had been intent only upon killing, for they had not eaten the mangled carcasses.

Athos stood in the kitchen distractedly stroking the head of a dead wood duck he held. Calmness and philosophy were required of me, I knew, but my words fell on deaf ears. Athos was inconsolable.

All morning he repaired the damage to the wire enclosure that we had thought would be so safe. I had never seen him in such a state; alternately he was livid with fury at the dogs and raging with anger at owners who would let murderous dogs roam at will or he was overcome with sorrow at the fate of his beautiful, trusting birds. He was so nauseated by the tragedy that he couldn't eat.

He was physically unable to paint in that state of mind and I, his wife, had to do something quickly. Just what I should do was elusive, beyond my vision. I was unequal to the situation. I was stupid in a crisis. I was not a proper wife for Athos. I was miserable.

It was regrettable that we lived on rented property, where we could never have the perfect setup for our birds.

That was it! I ran shouting to Athos, "This minute I am going to find our very own land, where nothing short of an act of God can happen to harm our birds!"

For the first time that day, Athos smiled.

Within half an hour I had stated to a real estate man what we wanted in the way of property. He said, "Mrs. Menaboni, I think I have just what you want," and took me to acreage not a mile distance from where we rented.

Instantly I knew that it was what I personally wanted, but I told him that we would have to let him know later if we wanted to buy the land.

I entered the house to find Athos disconsolately trying to paint. His heart was not in it— the first time I had seen him not feel like painting.

I announced, "I think that I have found our land!"

Athos laid aside his palette in excitement, a different man, as he said, "Let's go right now to see it!"

We drove the mile, and my tongue wagged the entire time, describing what he was to see. We no sooner stopped the automobile than Athos started streaking through the valley with me tagging along behind trying to keep up with him. After he had gone a hundred feet, seeing the wooded hills, the valley and the brook, he arrived at the enormous jutting boulder on the hillside that gave a dramatic feature to the land. Abruptly he stopped and said with finality, "We will buy it."

That morning I had seen him in the depths of despondency. That afternoon I saw him at the height of happiness. From a great calamity had come a great good.

The matter was settled for Athos and from that instant he owned the land. He left all the red tape to me, for he had slight interest in titles, deeds, recording at the courthouse, and money changing hands. He saw the land he wanted, and he owned it immediately.

He was preoccupied with what was most important to him, the safety of the birds. The next

morning he and a workman with rolls of wire fencing and posts started erecting a fence to keep predators off our six acres. Nothing else mattered to Athos except his objective to make an ideal place for his birds. I had scarcely finished attending to all the business pertaining to ownership, even the money payment, before Athos had the fence halfway around the acreage!

Our birds' welfare . . . A few minutes ago Athos called to me to come see the first purple finches that have come to our sanctuary. After the snow had ceased falling, he had cleared a place on the terrace upon which he placed grain for all the hungry birds that did not know about the feeding station. He had also placed there a terra-cotta bowl of warm water for them to drink.

I believe that the wood ducks will like coming here on Christmas.

December 21, and Athos has just passed my window, on the way to the valley to plant the two rosemary bushes we bought yesterday. Rosemary, for remembrance of the rosemary of Italy.

I recall the time that we wandered over the acres we had just purchased, absorbing their beauty and marveling that they were ours. We had an intense desire to begin working upon the

land, but where to begin? Ahead of us was a staggering amount of work and dozens of things had to be accomplished immediately, but what should be done first? What plan should we follow? We wanted to preserve the beauty that nature had provided, yet there were things we must do for its improvement, and we must make no mistakes. The unsightly dead logs must be cleared away, the half-rotten stumps dug out, the poison ivy and brambles removed, but the acreage was to be left as wild as possible on habitable ground.

We needed one open space in the woodland. The logical place for the clearing was a part of the valley, which showed signs of having been farmed only a few years ago, but which was now grown over in weeds and scrubby growth. It was there that Athos and his hired hands started, after Athos carefully explained that the thicket growth nearest the road was to be left intact as the ideal nesting site and cover for songbirds, and as a screen to ensure our privacy when we were in the valley.

To us, each plant merited attention, and we supervised every single thing done, although our Ike instinctively knew what we should like to have saved. We knew that it would be vandalish to let a gang of workmen loose on our hills and

Wood Duck

valley without watching them, for they would not appreciate mountain sumac, small dogwoods, buckeyes, ferns and moss. To their eyes these plants would be mere bushes and weeds to be trampled and destroyed. We insisted that they detour a carpet of foamflowers, and cautioned them not to step on the hundreds of bloodroots that dotted the hillsides. They probably thought we were crackpots, but today we have these plants as a feature of the place.

We were awed by the size of the property; six acres seemed at that time to be a hundred. The scope of the job we had to do bewildered me and I couldn't decide on a specific project to undertake personally first. I was not like Athos, who saw the place as a whole. I wanted to busy myself with some spot all my own, create a perfect little picture, and see the results of my labor quickly. I selected an area at the foot of the sloping hillside that I called "my rock garden," where there was a jutting rock as a nucleus around which to work. Days and days I spent upon the planting of wild flowers, vines, ferns, and moss. I fixed my rock garden to suit my taste in an area ten feet in diameter.

When it was finished I almost cried, for my work hardly showed at all. Ten measly feet in six acres!

Athos came to my rescue saying, "Forget all that must be done and just enjoy yourself."

They were the words he had used when I had been overwhelmed with my ignorance of birds and had wanted to learn all about them instantly. I must enjoy myself, and little by little everything would work out all right. That afternoon I found that there were many little ways in which I could make my contribution daily, without getting into a frenzy about moving mountains. The valley floor was being cleared of all except moss, so I rescued jack-in-the-pulpits, violets, foamflowers, ferns, and other small flora to transplant against the rock wall Athos was building. They snuggled there as if they had always been in that location,

and incidentally took away the new appearance of the wall. While exploring, I found some maidenhair ferns to plant where we could see them all the time. I enjoyed myself.

As I planted some willows beside the brook I remembered that on the property deeds this stream was named Brown Branch. I thought it an inappropriate name for my brook, which had its source in springs of clear water leaping over rocks and was bordered with gentians, lizard-tails, tiny wild irises, trefoil, wild geraniums, and hundreds of unknown plants. There were all the dogwoods I wanted and all the umbrella trees Athos wanted. Definitely I did not want our brook named Brown Branch. It had to be renamed, but what would suit my fancy? I remembered my favorite stream in the Italian Alps, and there seemed to be no reason why I should not rename my brook the Lys.

I looked over the shady valley, the valley of ever-moving shadows, that colorful autumn day. If it was my privilege to rename my brook, it was also suitable that the whole place should have a name. Athos was working close by, and I told him that we must give our acres an Italian name. I insisted that he start saying Italian names until I heard one that struck my fancy, and to humor me he began reminiscing of the happy summers during his childhood in Italy spent at Vall'Ombrosa.

Suddenly I remembered what John Milton had written:

Thick as autumnal leaves that strow the brooks
In Vall'Ombrosa, where th'Etrurian shades
High over-arch'd imbower.

There was our name, Valle Ombrosa. The name tied the present into the past for Athos. Now I, too, had a Valle Ombrosa in my life, right here in Atlanta, Georgia.

Milton had written of his Vall'Ombrosa in *Paradise Lost*. Ours is a paradise found.

CHAPTER EIGHT

To own Valle Ombrosa was a boon to Athos and a much-needed escape for him from the war news. He could become preoccupied with his work on the land and have some relief from the mental sickness brought on by the deplorable situation of his native country and his mounting anxiety over the welfare of his family in Italy. He would paint until he could no longer endure thinking about all the horrible things that might be happening to his mother and father, brother and two sisters, then he would say, "Sara, I must get to the land, quick!" After some minutes of digging in the earth, or hauling rocks for his walls, or carrying gallons of water to put on young plants, or pruning dead limbs from trees he would recover himself. Nature was his antidote for the poisons of war.

There were scarcely any birds at Valle Ombrosa that year. An occasional blue jay hurried past on his important business, some crows flew overhead, and sometimes a vulture swung high in the air. But there were no birds in our bushes and no birds in our trees. We kept hoping they would come. The fence would help and the "posted" signs. The planting for shelter, and escape from enemies, and nesting sites, and the plentiful food would in time make the birds learn that Valle Ombrosa meant Sanctuary.

Across the road was a beautiful creek that was bordered by thick vegetation—an ideal place for birds. Through brambles, masses of blackberries, and almost impenetrable wild bamboo we pushed our way to watch the birds. I asked them why they did not repay our visits and come over to Valle Ombrosa to see us sometime.

I remember a yellow-breasted chat that was easier to hear than to see because of his constant noisy chatter, but he preferred to stay in thick briery vegetation. I invited him to come over to my valley—but no, he was quite content where he was.

Then another day across the road we saw two male yellow-breasted chats fighting all around us, not separating because we were close by. I told them that there was no necessity of being pugnacious over that territory. Just across the road was land empty of birds and one of them could set up housekeeping at Valle Ombrosa.

Maybe a chat heard me, was lured by my enticing—to his doom. At our wire gate we found that a yellow-breasted chat had flown against the wire and had broken his neck. Athos picked up the dead bird and held it in his hands, saying, "Did he die in vain?"

I looked at Athos's hands. "With your hands holding a paint brush you can immortalize this bird, can't you?"

"I don't know about immortalizing the bird—but I will paint him." And that day he started the picture.

The birds seemed hesitant, as though waiting for something. What was wrong at Valle Ombrosa? We were working as hard as we knew how to make our acres attractive to them.

Finally a lone Kentucky warbler nested on the ground beneath some jack-in-the-pulpits. We were happy that one bird wanted to move into Valle Ombrosa—but her young ones were ill fated—they were destroyed by some predatory creature.

The birds seemed to be waiting. For what?

Our friends did not wait. It was amazing and gratifying to see them take an intense interest in Valle Ombrosa. On Sunday afternoons we had visitors at our "open house" and once we arrived late to receive our callers and found on the gate a formal calling card! We had many outdoor meals on our new land and many people helped us not only with advice but with labor.

One morning my father and mother came from Rome especially to see the land. Father gave us the benefit of his knowledge by telling us that the choked and barely trickling spring at the foot of a hill could be cleaned out and harnessed to give us a plentiful supply of water. That afternoon some friends joined us who had not seen Valle Ombrosa and I was amused to see my father showing them around as though it belonged to him. He said, "We will have the driveway wind up that hillside to where the house will be . . . we do not wish to plant grass that would have to be mowed in the cleared valley, so we are developing a sod of moss . . . we will fill up this gully by dumping debris into it, then we will make a sunken lily pool . . . here we will have another pool bordered by azaleas until later we can build a dam farther down the brook for a lake . . . we are putting these birdhouses up now, so the birds can see them and next year take up residence in them . . ." We—I liked it very much that everyone said "we."

The land had been purchased from William E. Arnaud, who took a special interest in the plans we had for developing Valle Ombrosa. He and his wife started giving us great quantities of shrubs, small trees, ivy, and anything at their home grounds for which we expressed a liking. They owned the houseless land adjoining Valle Ombrosa and also the property across the road where the creek was, and told us to enjoy those acres to the fullest extent. In countless ways they were magnificent neighbors so that Athos said, "It was worth buying Valle Ombrosa just to know the Arnauds."

Indeed, our hearts were filling up with so many friends that we hardly knew where to put them all; yet the more that came the more space we seemed to acquire to put them.

Molly and Dick Aeck also were excited over our new venture and entered into the spirit of it. As Dick was an architect, it came naturally that he should draw house plans for us. Athos, being a creative artist, knew that Dick should not be dictated to, but left to do his work free from too many stipulations. The result was a charming house plan, with a beautiful brick garage and bricked-in terrace.

With the blueprints in hand, the two men pointed out to me the exact building site. When they said it would be necessary to cut four or five large dogwoods, I protested vigorously. "Over my dead body you'll cut my dogwoods! Your problem is to plan around those dogwoods!"

After all I had asked for nothing previously, and Dick could afford to indulge his client. With quick strokes of his pencil on the blueprints he drew curving retaining walls, and my dogwoods were saved.

That first part of December, 1941, the architectural drawings were given to contractors to study and to make estimates as to how much the building would cost. But that first Sunday afternoon, as we were listening to the New York Philharmonic Orchestra, a voice broke into the radio broadcast to announce—Pearl Harbor!

I sat there stunned by the shock. War . . . I looked at Athos. Upon his countenance was an expression of the accumulation of sadness of all men since they were created. He made a typical Latin gesture with his shoulders, then looked straight into my eyes. "Come, Sara," he said as he arose from his chair and came to take my hand, "we go out to nature."

Two days after Pearl Harbor, amid all the hysteria and uncertainty, the contractors gave us their estimates on the cost of building. The estimates were sky-high, all out of proportion to our carefully planned finances. The birds had done very well by us, but they had not made us millionaires. We had to abandon the hope of a house of our own. There could be no haven for

Common Raven

the birds, and our morale was very low indeed.

We told Dick that we could not build our dream house. He was as sorrowful as we were, for he knew how much it meant to us to live at Valle Ombrosa, and naturally he had wanted to see the house he had planned become a reality. All of us tried to be philosophical, but we made a fizzle of it.

Again Athos and I went outdoors to nature, but sometimes nature seems slow about giving the answers; nature did not give us the bright idea until ten o'clock that night. Instead of building a house for the automobile, why not make that structure into a tiny guest house to live in until after the war? The automobile did not have to have a roof over its head, while we did!

With a Rebel yell, I ran to the telephone. Dick caught our enthusiasm and told us to hurry over to talk about new plans. I have never seen a couple of miles so long. Inspired, Dick threw all his artistry and resourcefulness into making a complete house within the limitations of twenty-five feet by twenty-five feet. Anyone with a million dollars could build a fine house, but Dick would make a perfect postage-stamp-sized house!

At the time Dick was developing the idea, he had no notion that his house would be described in a magazine. But in the November, 1946, issue of *The Perfect Home*, there is the following description of our home:

"If the talents of Architect Richard L. Aeck had been available to Thoreau when he retired to Walden, this guest house might have graced the shores of the world's most famous pond, and its merits would have been extolled on numerous pages of America's finest literature.

"Untrammeled comfort and unusual convenience have been attained with a functional plan which has sacrificed nothing of the warmth and beauty which we associate with the word 'home.' Here is a dwelling which, through the taste and temperament of its builder, has in itself become an essay on a way of living. Space limitations have been transformed by inventiveness to a positive attribute, and by its very compactness this home strikes a pleasant note of informality . . .

"The living room, featuring spacious windows, harmonious modern furniture, and a handsome fireplace, intimately invites occupancy. As a studio, it furnishes a wealth of natural light. As a dining room it fairly flatters the plainest meal by the sparkling beauty of the setting and an out-of-doors tang.

"Everything necessary to the art of successful loafing is provided by the neat bunkroom with its strategically located bookshelves, telephone, and drawer space.

"The tiny kitchenette, replete with modern appliances and tastefully arranged cupboards and shelves, adequately fulfills every culinary need. There is ample 'elbow room' and no wasted space."

No, Dick did not know that later the Menaboni house would be written about; nothing mattered to him or to us except to make a house at Valle Ombrosa.

On January 1, 1942, the house was started, a dream becoming a reality.

On May 1 we moved in at dusk. A good friend thoughtfully brought us some supper, and to make it a momentous occasion, a huge moon came up—a full moon—reflecting the fullness of our lives.

The next morning, in one of the dogwoods by my house that I had determinedly saved, a summer tanager started building her nest! Within a week, a red-eyed vireo nest was in another dogwood and a blue-gray gnatcatcher nest was in a hickory. All three nests were in a radius of ten feet from the house-that-birds-built. So that was what the birds had been waiting for—they had wanted us to move into Valle Ombrosa before they did!

We were not here long before we sensed that some subtle thing was lacking. Was it the blank space on the front of the brick house that needed ornamentation in addition to the newly planted ivy and Paul's Scarlet rose? What should we put in that space that would be exactly right, and have significance for a sanctuary?

The moment the inspiration came to Athos he started working with Georgia clay, molding with his hands a statue. We found a place where the statue could be fired and glazed, Athos made a little wooden pedestal to attach to the brick façade for the statue to stand upon, and over it put a small wooden roof for the trailing red rose. Our Guiding Spirit stood enshrined— St. Francis, the Patron Saint of the Birds.

When we moved in to live at Valle Ombrosa it was the signal for the birds to move in also, although for a year they had shunned the land. On May 2, in addition to the summer tanager busily building her nest, a white-breasted nuthatch came to walk up and down tree trunks; a Carolina wren explored a gully filled with debris as a possible nesting site; and a wood thrush brought his lady love to sing to. Soon we had three nesting pairs of wood thrushes, a ruby-throated hummingbird, and another red-eyed vireo nesting in a dogwood overhanging the driveway. That summer there were two successive families of bluebirds in one of the dozen nesting boxes we had provided, and as soon as these tenants moved out a chickadee moved in to raise her brood. In the thicket in the valley near the road were nests of a cardinal, a catbird, and an indigo bunting. A Carolina wren nested under a lumber pile and another under the eaves of the aviary. A sparrow hawk occupied a hole

in a dead pine at the property line, and not far distant over the border was a broad-winged hawk nest. Mourning doves were to be seen always on one hill, and pileated woodpeckers were around every day, which led us to believe that they had nests somewhere at Valle Ombrosa; eventually we saw the dove nest high in a pine, and eventually the pileated woodpeckers brought their lone child right up to our house for us to see. Now there was all this nesting, whereas the spring and summer before there had been the one nest only of the Kentucky warbler, and not another bird. Ah, yes, I must not fail to tell that another Kentucky warbler nested in the same place as in the previous season. Was she the same one returning to see if she could be successful in raising a brood this time? I am happy to report that she did! And when she had finished using her nest, Athos brought it and also the clump of jack-in-the-pulpits to the house to paint. (After he had finished the picture, he took the jack-in-the-pulpits back to replant in the same hole, for she might need them the next season.)

Athos made a feeding station out of bits of leftover wood and painted it to look like an old, weathered, bronze coach light. He placed it on a post outside one of our huge windows so that we could see it as we sat at our dining-room table. Trumpet honeysuckle and trumpet flower vines were planted to climb up the post and over the roof of the feeding station, not solely for the artistic effect but for nectar-filled flowers for hummingbirds, who could not eat the seeds and grains that other birds could find there. Another feeding station of a different type was made to hang upon a near-by tree limb, this one containing suet.

A week passed, and no birds ventured near the two feeding stations. When the third week came and no birds took the offered foods, I was beginning to despair. But Athos only laughed at my impatience, and went with peanut butter and stale doughnuts to add to the provisions on the stations. Then one day a Carolina wren went to a feeding station, closely followed by a female cardinal. Next in line was a Carolina black-

Eastern Bluebird

capped chickadee—all within fifteen minutes. Did they pass the word around that there was a free lunch awaiting any and all birds? From that time on, the birds came to help themselves. Even a chipmunk discovered that he could climb up the post, eat his fill from the tray and carry away cheek pouches full. We let him enjoy his feasts also, for there was plenty for all creatures.

There was a ground feeding station covered with a roof for the pets that we turned free inside our fenced-in grounds. The wild turkey hen found her nesting site beside a log in the thicket; the Canada geese found theirs at the far end of the valley above the pool; and the mallards got busy locating their nesting places. I have never seen such activity while we were all getting settled.

At the same time that the house was under construction Athos built a fine aviary for the species of birds that we had to keep caged. Actually the aviary was larger than our house. There were four divisions, and the species that would get along together were put in each. On top of the roof were two pigeon houses. "Why do you have ordinary pigeons?" a great many people asked. But when they heard for the first time the Javanese cow bell that a friend had got for us to put on the side of our house to call the pigeons to eat (and there has never been a more melodious dinner bell), they understood why we did not have to make a trip all the way to Venice to be surrounded by pigeons.

Not content with the great outdoors or the fine aviary, the birds invaded our wee house as well. All right, they had built it, they owned it; the fact that we lived there too was incidental. Orphaned or sick or wounded birds were all about the interior, the electric incubator was full of eggs in the bathroom, and likely as not some bird was occupying the shower-bath stall. The kitchen was very popular. Birds would be flying in to be fed, I would be preparing baby formulas there, or Athos would be getting from the refrigerator the raw meat for the hawks and owls, or robbing me of all the lettuce or cabbage. I do not recall that any critter has taken over our bunkroom for sleeping quarters, but since my desk is in the bunkroom (did someone say that here is "everything necessary to the art of successful *loafing*"?), many a bird has visited me while I write. A young flicker in particular liked me to be busy at my typewriter. At those times he could walk all over the machine and me, exploring with his long tongue. There was never a dull moment with such tenants.

Oh, yes, I forgot Athos's innumerable pots of cacti that he brings indoors during the winter. The house is not small enough, the house is not crowded enough with occupants; we also have spiny cacti pricking us at every turn!

Valle Ombrosa is not only a home for us, the birds, and the potted cacti, but for the animals: Yama, Zulu, Sussi and Biribissi, a chipmunk or two, a flying squirrel, and ever so many others, such as—no—I'll begin their story in another paragraph.

One night after we came home late from a party we discovered a white-footed mouse in the bathroom. How she got there was a mystery, since this species does not ordinarily inhabit houses. After examining the floor underneath the wooden slats in the shower stall, Athos found that she had just given birth to four babies. They were naked, with closed eyes, minute helpless things. The mama was frantic; she had thought she had moved into the perfect home for her babies, but instead, two huge monsters threatened their lives. Or did they?

In the middle of the night Athos got a wire cage, placed the family in it on a man-made cloth nest and provided them with food and water. They settled peacefully for the night, the babies' mouths attached to the breasts of their mother.

St. Francis, the Patron Saint of *all* creatures, even unglamorous, lowly mice, lives at Valle Ombrosa.

CHAPTER NINE

*A*T THE BEGINNING of this month I wondered how we should start off this New Year in a memorable way. In the stores everyone was taking inventories to determine with what to restock their half-empty shelves. How should we restock our shelves? Every so often an artist needs fresh inspiration; both Athos and I needed change and refreshment.

Since our marriage, Athos had taken me three times to his native Italy, but he had never taken me to the scene of his first American outdoor experience, nor on my own initiative had I been to the neighbor state of Florida. Since, little by little, Athos's past was assuming greater significance as the background for his present, I thought I would like to visit the second place Athos had lived in America, and tie it up with the present.

I hinted my desire. "Athos, there are many species of birds that winter in Florida, aren't there?"

"Yes, and there are some birds in Florida that can be seen nowhere else in the United States. I did not know this when I lived in Florida so soon after coming to this country, and I missed seeing some of the rare sights. But I know now what to go searching for. Let's go to Florida!"

We had to make important arrangements for the proper care of our birds and the ailing Zulu. Some kind friends said they would postpone their trip to California so that we could have our motor trip first, and assured us we need harbor no worries about Valle Ombrosa.

We were off early in a cold rain, and swathed in heavy woolens, but before the day was over the rain had stopped and we longed to be in summer clothes down where the cabbage palms and the oleanders and camellias were in bloom. The rain had prevented our seeing many birds, and we counted only sixteen species; but we did not worry about it, for we had two weeks ahead of us and should drive over two thousand miles. I knew I could fill up a notebook with the birds we should see.

As I now leaf through the pages of the notebook I kept carefully and accurately in diary form, I see that I dare not include here all those lists. They would mean little to others and only make me sound as crazy as a loon to have been so excited over them. Why should I have been so thrilled that first morning in St. Augustine when a couple of feet from the sea wall I saw a bird about the size of a small goose and not very pretty in his winter plumage? Why? Because it was the first time I had ever seen a common loon!

While crossing a bridge we were amused to see a gull atop each lamppost, as though a sculptor had put them there as living ornamentation. Why weren't they perturbed by the traffic? Why did the motorists behind us on the bridge honk their horns to make us drive faster?

I notice in my notes that I asked many questions.

As we were riding in comfort were we seeing the descendants of the tree swallows, coots, Florida gallinules, killdeers, shrikes, and other birds that Audubon and other early naturalists had seen while trudging afoot?

Why wasn't that male ground dove upon my hearth at Valle Ombrosa with my little lady?

Why did thirty-four ruddy turnstones fly to a pier with thirty-six cormorants and one herring gull when we wanted to see them closer?

Why did folk go to Hialeah Park to make racing bets of millions of dollars in one week when, without spending a cent, they could go there during the morning to see the hundred and fifty or more pinioned flamingos taking the sun, their rosy-vermilion reflections mirrored in the still lagoon water?

Miami Beach was a snare and a delusion for bird lovers, for we tried for miles to find a spot on the beach without mobs of sun bathers; not a bird could wedge itself on that beach anywhere. Finally we saw a lone brown pelican on a fishing pier, and we came as close as five feet to him. It was evident that he was hanging around waiting to be fed a fish, but the men were having no luck. We decided to hang around also, for it would be some time before we could have a seafood lunch.

Good! A fisherman caught a three-pounder, but the pelican and we had a letdown feeling when the man wrapped the fish in paper. When the pelican edged closer, the fisherman chased him away. In a few minutes he was back, watching his opportunity with keen eyes and a don't-care manner to fool the men.

Athos and I stayed motionless and silent, wondering whether or not the pelican could steal that fish when all backs were turned. Slowly, little by little, the pelican stole forward; and we were breathlessly hoping that no one else would notice. Quickly he lunged, grabbed the paper—and we were feeling pretty good about it when—drat it, a girl screamed the alarm! The pelican had to fly away without his lunch. Why don't some folk understand that pelicans have to eat too?

As we walked on the Clearwater beach, we, like other people, collected shells, but I did not notice that those other beachcombers collected bird data as we did. We watched the behavior of several gulls as they flew over the beach with some sort of clam in their bills, dropped it on the sand to break the shell, and then alighted to eat the morsel from the broken shell. If the shell had not been broken by the impact with the sand, it was picked up, borne aloft again and once more dropped. Smart birds.

We found several cypress swamps, and had a delightful time poking amid cypress knees to find water plants we could collect to bring to Valle Ombrosa. We felt that we had the wilderness all to ourselves.

We were having a perfect winter holiday, doing exactly what we wished, filling up our minds with the birds we wanted, seeing only a few persons who shared our same interests. I remembered what William Bartram had written when parting with a mechanic who had been his fellow traveler: "Our views were probably totally opposite: he seemed to be actuated by no other motives than to establish his fortune. Whilst I, continually impelled by a restless spirit of curiosity, in pursuit of new productions of nature, my chief happiness consisted in tracing and admiring the infinite power, majesty, and perfection of the great Almighty Creator, and in the contemplation, that through divine aid and permission, I might be instrumental in discovering, and introducing into my native country, some original productions of nature, which might become useful to society."

We spent a memorable morning in the private garden of the modern plant explorer, Dr. David Fairchild, who has collected flora from all over the world to introduce into his native country for the use of society. The enthusiasm of this naturalist was so contagious that I felt a rekindling of zeal for the natural wonders of the world. As we went about the garden, I could see that Athos was restocking his shelves, taking in a fresh supply from the Florida storehouse he had discovered during his first years in America, and adding the species of plants Dr. Fairchild had brought from foreign lands. I looked at both men who had been so many places and done so many things. Were they talking about *themselves?* No, the conversation was entirely of nature, until they became excited over learning that they shared the same young protégé, a botanical painter, whom they had both inspired and

Northern Flicker

for whom they had opened the doors that led him to Guatemala to paint flora!

Dawn on the Tamiami Trail. We had left Miami before sunrise for a purpose: to be well in the Everglades as the birds awakened and started feeding. The friend who had planned our whole trip for us had insisted that we start out in the dark, so that we should not miss seeing a single bird and all the birds of this area, "that would take Athos a million years to paint."

Suddenly we saw ghost wings—an owl?— then a flying night heron; but there was not enough light to distinguish whether it was a yellow-crowned or a black-crowned. As visibility came, a coot could be plainly seen, then a pied-billed grebe, and we correctly identified a black-crowned night heron. Suddenly the sun was up over the horizon.

The automobile idled along, for we were in no hurry. We were in a wildlife refuge of two or three million acres that included the bulk of the Everglades, south of the Tamiami Trail, and taking in the Bay of Florida and Whitewater Bay. There was no trace of white civilization in this wilderness except the straight road, the canal on one side, and occasional stretches of so-called Australian pines that had been planted alongside the road.

Although there were no other evidences of white people, several times we came upon the thatched huts of small communities of Seminole Indians, seeing them at first asleep on their open platforms. When they were up and about their business, they never cast a glance at our passing automobile. I had been told by many people in Florida that "there is nothing to do for or about the Seminoles," as they have never come under the rule of the United States government, and, furthermore, do not want any meddling or assistance from any private person or organization. Yet seeing their pitiful plight never failed to make me mentally ill. As an American, I can be proud and satisfied over how much is being done today to protect birds and animals; as an American, I am ashamed of the existing condition of the Seminoles. I console myself with the thought that at least in the Everglades they have a place to live.

Now I was beginning to see birds thick and fast: dozens of coots in the canal; crows, sparrow hawks, and kingfishers perched singly on vantage points above the canal that was alive with fish. We saw twenty black vultures perched on some boulders by the canal, but we stopped counting turkey and black vultures, for they were in vast numbers. Next came a Florida gallinule, marsh hawk, several American egrets, and great blue heron after great blue heron (we saw only a few little blue herons); then a huge flock of boat-tailed grackles. Near a small truck farm (how did this farm manage to be in this refuge?) were two mockingbirds and several bluebirds perched on telephone wires. Farther along we saw three red-winged blackbirds, a green heron on a rock by the water, a cormorant, and a flock of tree swallows. Woodpeckers had been conspicuously absent, but a red-bellied woodpecker put in his appearance.

We came to cypress forests, the tree trunks covered with clusters of air plants, one with open red flowers that stood out as a bold splotch of color in the gray-green landscape. Often the canal was choked with water hyacinths. These make a beautiful sight when in bloom, but are the despair of Floridians, who try in vain to keep their waterways cleared of this introduced plant. The banks of the canal held many flowers unknown to us until we saw a bloom we could name, the lowly thistle.

In the distance we saw great numbers of American egrets and snowy egrets flying together. The sight of these two types of white-plumaged birds was what I had been told made the Tamiami Trail so interesting. I was pleased that we could take our time and not have to speed toward some

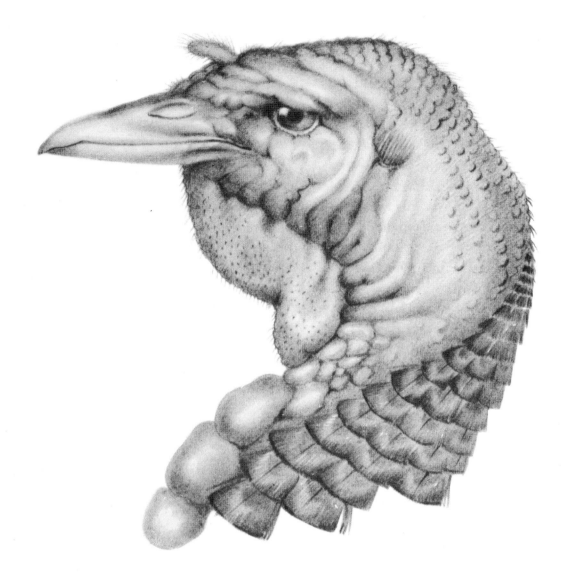

destination. As a tourist and bird lover, I was ready for my share of egrets.

I had been instructed also in this identification. The gracefully shaped American egrets have pure-white feathers; the bill is chrome-yellow as well as the lores, the latter, however, being tinged with green; and, very important to know, the legs and feet black. The snowy egret is smaller than the American egret, white-plumaged, but with a black bill yellow at the base and the lores yellow; and although the legs are black, the toes are yellow.

As we got close to them and stopped the automobile, they stretched their long white necks high in alarm, then they took off in flight— glittering white against the cerulean sky. Small wonder that man's imagination has endowed heavenly angels with great white outspread wings! There was no Angel of Death here in the Everglades; all were alive and fearing no evil in their millions of acres of wilderness given to them by the grace of God—and the United States government.

In the automobile I had the publication of the U.S. Department of Agriculture, *Florida, National Forests*, and read snatches of the early days in Florida's history: "Florida's memories are many-colored, for every manner of man has walked through the pages of her history. Cavaliers and grandees in Spanish galleons sought bullion and gold. Pirates and free-booters sacked and plundered with oaths and bloodshed. Black-robed priests marched up and down in mission gardens reciting their breviaries . . . Peril and strife and hardship have passed, and the succeeding centuries have seen the creation and growth of a new empire from the unbroken forests Ponce de Leon discovered in 1513. Man has pushed back the forests, but they have resisted even the fury of war and the white man's greed. The million and a half acres of national-forest lands in Florida have been part of the background of four centuries of colorful history . . . They have survived the era of discovery, the adventures of immigration, the pressure of exploitation, and the demands of industrialism . . . The forest land in Florida has been cut over or culled. The virgin forests of today are mostly in the swamps, and under improved economic conditions these are rapidly being harvested."

The virgin forests, harvested. But white men had not been able to do anything with the millions of acres of the Everglades, and had left them to the birds. Oh! Oh! milady liked to have aigrettes on her hat, and the millinery trade demanded that great numbers of egrets be slaughtered for their plumage, until bird lovers and conservationists stepped in to end that harvesting of wildlife for vanity and financial greed.

What excitement we experienced as we saw streaming over us five or six hundred white ibis! Their entire plumage was white, except the tips of their primaries, which were blackish, and their legs and feet were red. We stopped the automobile, to be screened beneath Australian pines, and watched the ibis flying so low over us that we could hear the whistle of the wind through their forty-inch wings. While we stood there awed, not less than six thousand white ibis went over us in that streaming flock, white against the sky. Our friend had been right; Athos could

never paint them all in a million years, but in a few minutes he could get all that he aesthetically desired.

Interests were coming so fast that there was no time for relaxing our guard. There now appeared a mixed flock of white ibis and American egrets, American egrets—American egrets, and still more American egrets! We had so many of them that we felt we had more than our rightful quota, and would have liked to share some hundreds with other persons. On and on we saw the egrets and ibis, elegant, fantastic, incredible. I became almost sated with seeing them, yet each time I squealed with excitement. I was storing them up in memory, so that if I forgot some thousands, still there would be other thousands to remember. That morning was all that Athos had remembered the Everglades to be and all he had hoped for my first time there.

And then we came to a pool rimmed entirely by statuesque, white-plumaged egrets and ibis. I shall never again appreciate marble statues quite as much as I did those living splendid birds. My apologies to sculptors; my gratitude to nature.

A St. Louis friend joined us for a day on the Florida Keys. We drove along the miles and miles of marshland dotted with hammocks and with an occasional glimpse of the ocean on our way to Tavernier. Sandwiched between our conversations about our St. Louis friends, I listed in my notebook nineteen species of birds and seventy-two individuals. Friends and birds galore; I do not know what more Athos and I desire, unless it is more friends and more birds! But our day was just beginning.

At Tavernier we boarded the boat with the appropriate name, *Spoonbill*, and Warden Eifler greeted us warmly. We had received permission from the National Audubon Society to go on this Audubon boat for a day with Mr. Eifler. His work is the protection of all the birds in an area of the Bay of Florida, but more especially the roseate spoonbills, which were almost extinct in Florida until the National Audubon Society took steps to save them. As Mr. Eifler saw my notebook, he said that, although he would tell me the names of the islands we should see, he did not wish me to record their names as it might make it easy for someone to come there hunting spoonbills or their eggs. Six years ago someone, for the fun of it, had shot six of these rare birds, not caring whether the gorgeous creatures became extinct or not.

The water itself was interesting in the Bay of Florida; it was opague light green, different from any we had seen. The milky water was not very deep; often we churned up the clayey bluish-white marl from the ocean floor, and once we were barely able to cross a "bank." Mr. Eifler said that the Bay of Florida here was not affected by the tides; however, because of the wind, the depth might vary as much as six inches. We had not been on a boat in such a long time that had the day not offered us anything else but this boat trip, Athos and I would have been satisfied.

Right away we saw a great white heron, the first we had ever seen! It was approximately the size of the great blue heron, but to me it looked even larger. Its pure white feathers make it extremely outstanding, whereas the great blue heron more or less blends with its background and is less conspicuous. This white bird, with its wingspread of eighty-three inches, was sitting atop some mangroves, at first motionless but, as we neared, off it went in deliberate, graceful flight. Audbuon had first seen the great white heron in 1832, and now Athos and I had come a thousand miles to see this species which today is to be seen practically nowhere except on the Florida Keys, although one may see an occasional straggler elsewhere in lower Florida. Mr. Eifler told us that, through protection, the species had increased from about three hundred in number to about a thousand. During the day we saw many of these beautiful birds, and I was glad that we

had not gone on a foreign expedition but were concentrating upon seeing our own rare continental birds.

We saw a bald eagle flying right over the water. Of course we saw many brown pelicans and cormorants, but we paid little attention to them, for we were eager to see the spoonbills, which were now nesting. Indeed, this locality is the only place in Florida where they nest. Mr. Eifler said that there are perhaps two hundred spoonbills at the present time. We neared a key rimmed with sand with mangroves standing in the water on tiptoe roots. We were all tense with expectation.

Suddenly Athos sighted a roseate spoonbill! Then our friend saw it and, lastly, in a stew of frantic searching, I saw it. Mr. Eifler laughed at our excitement, telling us that we should see lots more; but I shall never forget that one spoonbill. Seeing it at a distance through field glasses, so that I was not conscious of the flattened spatula-like bill or the bare head, I was aware only of the superb rose-pink color with touches of carmine.

I had seen American and snowy egrets and white ibis before, though not in such enormous numbers as on the Tamiami Trail. So far in Florida I had seen my first loon, first flamingo, first great white heron, and now a roseate spoonbill.

But now there was another species new to us —a reddish egret. I am afraid that I should have mistaken it in the distance for a little blue heron had not our friend pointed out that it was larger than the little blue and had a much heavier bill. It was running in a peculiar way in the shallow water getting its food. Later we saw a few more of these now rare birds.

A Louisiana heron, an osprey around its nest —these were worth noting; but the little flock of spoonbills nesting in the southeast exposure fascinated us most. Reluctantly we left them, to go churning up the marl toward other keys. We were certainly getting our birds this day. There was still another new species for Athos and me, a red-breasted merganser, and as we went on our way we saw nine of them flying together.

Again the engine was cut off as we neared a key and we glided silently toward the spoonbills, great white herons, reddish egrets, Louisiana herons, a little blue heron, three white ibis wading, and two yellow-crowned night herons flying about three feet above the water. These birds were being indelibly imprinted upon Athos's memory and right then, in a few minutes' time, I saw him painting all these birds at once. This was a particularly good place to see these birds, and our guide gave us plenty of time with them. To oblige us, four roseate spoonbills and three white ibis flew together against the blue sky— pink and white visions floating in the heavens!

Eventually, to lure us from this favored key, Mr. Eifler said, "Let's go see if the eagles are home." With this prospect, we were not loath to leave.

Sure enough we saw the female bald eagle sitting on the huge nest made of sticks. Her mate was not far away, sitting proudly and alertly on the most prominent limb of the tree. Athos and I had never been so close to nesting eagles, but Mr. Eifler said that he did not like to see them so tame for fear someone would get close enough to shoot them. Mind you, the bald eagle is protected by law, but the previous season someone had taken a shot at a pair, scaring them away from their nesting activities. It is impossible to believe that there are people who would like to kill the American emblem bird! The male resented our presence and screamed at us, so we left them in peace.

Mr. Eifler patrols about forty miles, and we had an afternoon of birds and more birds, exactly what we had set out from Atlanta to have. I believe we were most impressed by the roseate spoonbills, in spite of our determination never to be partial to any one species. Thirty roseate spoonbills in flight at once against the azure sky,

with the milky-green water below them, was an ethereal picture that I never expect to see duplicated. Nor shall I ever forget the exquisite picture at another key of about eighty-five "pinks" like great blossoms on the trees.

As we neared the last key on our return to Tavernier, I, an insatiable mortal, complained to Mr. Eifler that he had promised to show me another new species to add to my bird list, the man-o'-war birds, and that he had failed me.

He laughed at my greed. "Maybe I am saving something for the last."

He kept his promise, as a grand climax to our day. Graceful in flight, with their long arched wings and forked tails, and dark against the sunset sky were twenty-seven man-o'-war birds.

In Florida, William Bartram wrote in 1774: "I listened, undisturbed, to the divine hymns of the feathered songsters of the grove, whilst the softly whispering breezes faintly died away. The sun now below the western horizon, the moon majestically rising in the east; again the tuneful birds became inspired: how melodious is the social mock-bird! The groves resound the unceasing cries of the whip-poor-will; the moon about an hour above the horizon; lo! a dark eclipse of her glorious brightness came slowly on; at length, a silver thread alone encircled her temples: at the boding change, an universal silence prevailed."

It was midmorning when Athos and I walked into a quiet grove outside Lake Wales. Enjoying this sanctuary with us were robins and jays. Ah, a sociable mockingbird came and perched on a tree to pour out his melodies to us, close enough that we could hear his breathing between notes.

On the pool was reflected the famous Singing Tower, beautifully fashioned of pink marble, reaching to the blue sky and holding carrillon bells that await a musician who will make them ring out in glory. Swimming in and out of the reflection of the tower were wood ducks in their

glorious array of colors, also mirrored in the water. As we sat amid the silence of the live oaks, hearing nature's melodies, watching the birds, seeing the magnificent handiwork of men, I contemplated the glories that were mine, all mine.

We experienced a boding change—which did not bring an universal silence, though it silenced the mockingbird, who hurried away to another haven—as we heard a great buzz of voices, and the grove became peopled. The spell was broken for us, and Athos wanted to leave, but I insisted that we stay to hear the carillon program. Following the printed instructions, we went some distance away from the tower to hear to best advantage the music of the bells, but a noisy airplane came to circle over the tall tower twice, drowning out the music of the bells—spoiling the music I had come from afar to hear, and desecrating the sanctuary. The plane left. Again the bells played clear, the music resounding from the tower as though by magic.

Two vultures lazily circled the tower, wheeling in fluid motion, adding to the beauty instead of marring it as the airplane did. Birds—vultures, yes—but adding immeasurably to the loveliness. I made a vow to my vultures that when

I returned to Atlanta I would write about them too.

Suddenly both of us were overcome with the longing to go back home to our own bird sanctuary, our little house snuggled on the hillside; to Yama, to Zulu (how was our sick marmoset getting along?), and to our friends. At the very same moment we said, "Let's hurry back to Valle Ombrosa!"

We could have stayed away two days longer, but something prompted us to hurry. We stopped only once, to pick up from the road a dead pig that had been killed by another automobile, feeling somewhat sorry that we were robbing the vultures of a meal. But, then, we had to carry a present to Valle Ombrosa to—but wait, that story will come later! We sped home, and there found out what had urged us to come that day: a supper party made up of intimate friends was in progress. It was a wonderful ending to our trip.

In January we had received, and we lost. We had half expected the news; therefore we were not surprised when we were told that Zulu had passed away in his sleep the night before our arrival. We were touched by the sympathy of our friends, who well knew that Zulu had been a member of our "family" and could never be replaced. They too had known him the fifteen years he had lived with us, and knew that our house would seem empty when we returned to it. A personality was gone, to marmoset heaven.

The couple who had taken care of Valle Ombrosa for us showed us motion pictures that they had taken here the year before. There on the screen appeared Zulu, frisky and happy. I smiled to see him alive once more. That is the memory I shall retain of our marmoset, just as through my memory run the beautiful motion pictures of all the Florida birds I saw with such happiness.

Belted Kingfisher

CHAPTER TEN

*T*HIS MORNING I am reminded of the lines of Coleridge:

He prayeth best, who loveth best
All things both great and small;
For the dear God, who loveth us,
He made and loveth all.

Of all the pictures we could have had to occupy the most prominent wall in our tiny house, we chose to have a painting of the turkey vulture over our fireplace. Why? We want it there. If I said that I wanted a golden pheasant picture, a mandarin duck picture, or a painting of a beautiful bird of any species, Athos would humor me and paint what I should want to fill that wall space. I have only to say the word and I can have any bird painted for my personal satisfaction—any bird! But we choose to have a turkey vulture picture. I am not sure that I should say the vulture is an aesthetically beautiful bird, but I am positive that the more I look at my picture the more I like my buzzard.

No matter what people may think of vultures, it has been amusing to witness their reactions to our turkey vulture picture. I have not heard a single person say that this picture is repulsive to him. Quite the contrary. I have lost count of the number who have said, "I should like to feel those feathers—run my fingers under them." Maybe that is one reason why we like the picture in our living room, to force sentiment for the vulture from those who have despised the living counterpart. I like to think that St. Francis had a hand in deciding what bird should be the focal point of our interior decoration.

I go back to the time when Athos and I went outdoors one day after a summer shower, and the leaves dripped prismatic drops upon us in the sunshine. A turkey vulture glided to a perch on a dead pine not fifty feet from us. After settling himself, he shook his body and proceeded to take a sun bath. He lifted his water-logged wings in spread-eagle fashion or let the wing feathers droop half-opened; occasionally he turned to let the sun rays reach a different portion of his body. He completely ignored our presence, and Athos had the opportunity to study him through field glasses for half an hour before the bird took off for the heavens.

Athos came indoors to draw the large bird exactly as he had observed it. This painting followed one which Athos had made of a bald eagle, and he remarked that the wings were almost identical in the two birds. The specimen-skin that Athos had was of a young turkey vulture, with grayish fuzz on the neck and head. The neck and head were not so bright red as a full adult's, but had a bluish cast. The painting was of a profile of the bird, and it was interesting to note that we could look right through the opening of the large nostrils, the maxilla being pierced. The eyes of the vulture were a soft brown. Athos enjoyed painting this bird as much as he has ever enjoyed painting more obviously attractive ones; indeed, he said that the vulture *was* beautiful.

I recall that on the trip to Florida there was something ludicrous in the sight of the many sodden vultures perching in trees during the rain. They appeared grotesque, like living gargoyles. It ceased to be mirthful when reason got the better of me and I recognized that those gawky birds were wet, cold, and hungry. They had to endure their misery stoically until the sky cleared, their feathers dried, and there were sufficient air currents for their flight so that they could climb high in the sky to scan for food below, while I was comfortable in an automobile

125

and knew that money could buy me a meal at any time I wished. As we went a few miles farther, we saw in a ditch alongside the road a dead cow offensive to human sight. I thanked God that soon our beneficial friends, the vultures, would remove that sight from the highway. The next time I saw vultures, I wished to tell them that a free lunch was awaiting them back a few miles. Not that they needed any telling, for by either sight or smell (the scientists disagree as to whether one or the other sense is employed, or both) they quickly find their waiting meals.

One day while driving along the miles of straight road in south Georgia, Athos and I looked for an interesting spot at which to stop and eat our picnic lunch. From one o'clock on, no place attracted or suited our fancy; two-thirty came and we were getting hungrier by the minute, but refused to stop until we could find a scene of more than passing interest. Suddenly Athos jammed on the brakes. While we sat on the running board eating our ham sandwiches, we observed half a dozen vultures on the road eating a dead pig that someone had run over. We were all eating the same kind of meat, only ours was cured and tenderized, cooked and spiced, and placed between slices of bread spread with mustard! I did not observe that the vultures turned up their noses in revulsion at the way we "civilized" creatures ate our pork.

Another time Athos and I deeply regretted that a laughter-provoking sight we saw was not recorded upon motion-picture film. That afternoon we saw a group of vultures on the hill opposite us so filled to capacity with their feast that they were unable to take off from the ground. They stumbled around like drunks, tried to leap, and fell back to the earth on wobbly feet. They struck ridiculous poses in their predicament, making running starts, futile jumps, and then falling plop! back to the ground. The gluttons were not capable of going to their night

roosting place, and as darkness closed upon them they were still stupidly trying to leap into the air that would not buoy up their weight. I have never seen in nature a performance to equal that comical sight, but maybe it wasn't so funny to the actors.

As I said, vultures were cheated of a meal when, on the way back from Florida, we picked up a little pig that some automobile had killed. We brought it to Valle Ombrosa as a gift to . . .

I think I had better go back to the beginning of this story. It will answer in still another way the question that is invariably asked by everyone we meet for the first time: "How long does it take to paint a bird picture?" This story, then, will give some idea of how long it took a certain picture to come into being. It is infinitely more important, however, as an instance of how people enter into the picture of our lives.

One day we received a letter from an unknown sergeant stationed at Fort MacPherson, just outside Atlanta, who was working as an entomologist, although in civilian life he had studied ornithology. He had seen Mr. Menaboni's bird pictures and would like to meet the artist. But perhaps he should get a formal introduction from one of the ornithological professors at Cornell University?

We do not like formality. Cornell was "way up yonder" in New York State. I wrote to the sergeant that all that was necessary for him to do was to telephone us and set a time when he could come to Valle Ombrosa. The following Sunday afternoon he came. We dismissed formality at once, and right away started swapping bird lore.

In the course of the conversation, the sergeant said that he had written an article about a golden eagle he had once had, and he asked if Athos had ever had a living eagle? When Athos answered in the negative, he told us how sorry he had been to have to refuse an offer from the San

Diego Zoo of a young golden eagle, because he was just at that time entering the service. Did Athos want the eagle, if it was still available? Imagine asking Athos if he *wanted* a golden eagle!

Our new friend wrote to the director of the San Diego Zoo about the matter, who answered that the golden eagle would be given to Athos if he would pay the transportation costs. Imagine asking Athos *if* he would pay the express charges!

When the express company notified me over the telephone that the crated eagle had arrived in Atlanta, I drove blithely into town to fetch our new bird. But after I saw the size of the roomy crate, my heart sank; there was no possible way to put it into the automobile or tie it on. I should have to get a delivery truck.

The sympathetic expressman started calling transfer companies for me. The reply he got was: "The OPA will not let us deliver that far into the country. It is out of our zone." Company after company he telephoned, in vain. The expressman was beginning to feel very sorry for me, and I was becoming frantic. Here was a

127

bird, the like of which we had never expected to own, but which Providence had sent our way. He had crossed the entire continent and now there was no way of getting him transported a measly fourteen miles to Valle Ombrosa. Something was vitally wrong in the setup.

The expressman called the number of the last transfer company in the telephone book, then quickly handed the receiver to me, saying, "You see if you have any luck!" I am a long-winded talker, and I gave my spiel so fast and pleadingly that the man at the other end of the line had no chance to insert a hasty "No." Finally he interrupted me: "Listen, lady, let me say a word, will you? Just where is Cook Road?"

I told him, and he said that he lived not far from me. We began chatting about the neighbors we both knew, how much we liked the section in which we lived, and at long last he said, "This evening I am taking a load of pipes to my home on my truck. I'll put the eagle box on top of the pipes and route my way home via your house and drop off the eagle for you."

I wanted to shout in sheer gratitude but I only thanked him for getting me out of a fix.

When the man arrived at Valle Ombrosa with the eagle, he was so interested in our birds and enjoyed himself so much that he did not want a fee for the delivery, and we had to force it upon him.

Through the wire we could see the huge bird, with fierce eyes and menacing-looking talons. Frankly, I was afraid. Athos admitted that two persons would be necessary to handle the strong bird, so I telephoned to the sergeant to come help take the eagle from the crate, since he had had experience in handling eagles.

My fear had been unjustified, for all John and Athos had to do was wrap the eagle in a leather jacket while they put jesses on the legs, attached a chain to these specially fashioned leather straps, and fastened the chain, which had a swivel, to a post. It might be a simple matter for people with experience, but I noticed that they worked with hands encased in heavy leather gloves. What kept the procedure from being difficult or really dangerous was that the eagle was already tame.

After the eagle was settled and beginning to get his bearings, we discussed how we were going to feed him. In a separate little box the San Diego Zoo had put two live guinea pigs, with instructions for the trainmen to kill them on certain days in transit. But after they had killed one and it had not been eaten, they used good sense in not offering the other. The sergeant suggested that he bring a mate for the guinea pig, then guinea pigs could be raised for eagle-food. The following Sunday he brought the guinea pig from the Medical Laboratory, and thus began a new experience for us, for we'd never had guinea pigs at Valle Ombrosa. Also, he brought three dead rabbits that had been used for experimental purposes. He said that he would continue to bring rabbits until the guinea pigs multiplied in sufficient numbers, for he felt a joint ownership-responsibility for the eagle.

That day a girl was here who asked, "What will you name the eagle?"

I told her that she could name him for us.

She thought for a few minutes, looked at the sergeant's uniform insignia, and said: "Since he got the eagle for you, let's name him 'The Sergeant'—Sarge for short." (Later, when our friend was promoted to a lieutenant, the Sarge retained his former rank.)

The Sergeant was not happy. He refused to eat the rabbits or anything else offered to him. We worried considerably during the two weeks he fasted until finally he decided to eat. He did not learn to go inside his house during rain or the hot midday, but stayed on his outside post, or flew the length of the chain. It was not pleasant for us to watch him from our windows in this unhappy state, angrily chewing at the leather jesses that he knew fettered him. The Sergeant

Snowy Egret

did not like dogs, and Yama kept a respectful distance from this king of birds. However, when we approached him, he was not afraid of us, ate from our hands, and would let us scratch the back of his neck.

One day Athos was painting and happened to look out the window toward the eagle outside. In a mad scramble, he ran to the door, yelling to me, "The eagle has got loose!"

I dashed to the door, then stopped still in my tracks as I saw Athos make a football player's lunge at the eagle on the terrace wall as the bird was about to spring into the air. My thought was: Athos's hands will be torn to shreds—what is the doctor's telephone number?

In a split second, Athos had grabbed both the legs at the same time, and was holding them tight, with the talons away from his body. As calmly as you please, Athos held the Sarge in his arms and I let out a sigh of relief.

As per instructions, I carried the leather jacket to Athos and helped wrap the eagle in it. Then we stood for ten minutes discussing what to do next. The Sergeant did not struggle; patiently he waited for us to make the decision not to put jesses on him again, and to abandon the special eagle-house that had been built for him by the wall of the front terrace and which he had disliked from the first.

I chased some silver Sebright bantams from one of the "rooms" of the aviary, and the Sergeant was put there. He liked it! No more jesses on his legs, a nice roof to get under during rain and hot sun, a suitable perch, lots of room in which to fly. He made himself at home.

Never again could we scratch the back of his neck, but we could go into his cage whenever we wished. He allowed photographers to enter, but he did not enjoy the procedure of being photographed by strangers. After many such experiences, one day the Sarge got tired of everybody crowding into his cage chasing him around to get him in good photographic positions. It was

as though he said aloud, "I'm going to put a stop to this," for he raised his head feathers in anger —the danger signal, which Athos recognized— and made a motion that indicated he was about to attack. Athos said, "We must scram!" and we cleared out of the cage in record time!

The Sergeant realized his triumph, for the next day he did the same trick to clear photographers out of his private domain. No more strangers in his lair! They could look at him through the wire, and he would show off his seven-foot wingspread, but they had to respect his rank by not being too familiar. Athos and I could enter his cage, yes, for we were home folk, but no one else.

Of course by now you have guessed that the dead pig we brought home from our trip to Florida was for the Sarge. Food for him was a real problem during wartime rationing of meat; besides, meat from the butcher was not a proper diet all the time. Our friends entered into the spirit of the hunt, and it was amazing what a quantity of rabbits, squirrels, and oppossums could be found dead on roads. However, the last-named were not relished, and I informed the fortune-hunting friends not to get possum any more. Mind you, all this was during gasoline rationing also, and our friends used their precious gas to drive to Valle Ombrosa, or I used ours to go miles for the prizes. Everyone had problems and we managed somehow; every morning the Sergeant wanted his breakfast, and no fooling.

Shortly after we got the eagle, some friends who knew we had open house every Sunday afternoon, brought their out-of-town visitors to Valle Ombrosa. Right then a Long Island couple fell in love with the Sergeant and asked Athos to paint a portrait of the bird.

They had to wait a year and a half for the picture. Athos studied the bird in a thousand poses, sketched him in the cage, and while painting the actual picture, returned time after time to look at the coloration. When the picture was finished, our friends came to Atlanta again. After they had seen it, they insisted that we must have a dinner party downtown, and hurriedly assembled our mutual friends to celebrate that night. With champagne, we drank a toast: "To the Sergeant!"

It is hard to answer the question, "How long does it take to paint a bird picture?" It is not a matter of how many days Athos works at his easel. I believe it would be more pertinent to ask: "What goes into a Menaboni bird picture?"

And this is not the kind of story that ends abruptly, for today I am paying a price in loneliness for the Sergeant's sake. Athos has gone off for the day hunting with a friend to try to get some rabbits for the Sergeant. The food problem is always with us.

This morning I am reminded of a story that goes something like this: The Poverello of Assisi, after hearing the villagers' tale of woe about a wolf destroying their sheep and, worse than that, eating their children, persuaded the men not to go kill the wolf, and said he would go outside the village walls to talk the matter over with the beast. In fear and trembling the townsmen watched St. Francis calmly approach the ferocious animal saying, "Brother wolf, why are you a killer?"

The wolf answered that he could find food in no other way, but that if he were regularly fed by the people of the village he would do them no more harm. St. Francis promised the wolf

that food would be set out every day for him. The promise was kept, and never again was there trouble.

Formerly I thought this story farfetched, but now I do not think it so improbable.

Let me go back to the day when Athos and I chanced upon a wounded female red-tailed hawk. Obviously someone had shot her, yet she had escaped with only a broken wing. Helpless on the ground, she would have died of starvation had we not come along. Her eyes were fierce, and she had just cause to hate human beings. At the sight of us she lay on her back, terrified, brandishing her feet with the long talons in the air. She knew that her only method of defense would be to tear our flesh.

Athos threw his leather jacket over her and in a moment had wrapped her securely in it. He held her legs firmly, and before we reached Valle Ombrosa she had ceased struggling. She behaved nicely while her wounds were swabbed with antiseptic, a splint was applied to hold the broken bones in place, and both wings were tied to her body to keep her from flapping them.

While she was "taking the cure," it was imperative that she be put in a warm, enclosed spot with not too much light, and that she see us often enough so that she would recognize us as her friends. In our tiny house there was not much choice as to where she could be put—of course the shower-bath enclosure! Once there, terror and hate left her eyes and were supplanted by curiosity and wonder. We gave her a piece of meat and left her alone, to get her bearings in peace.

Within three days she was eating out of our hands. She found that we meant no harm when we scratched the back of her head and neck and smoothed her breast feathers, and she closed her eyes, apparently in ecstasy when we petted her. She learned to ride on our gloved hands to the kitchen when we wanted the shower bath to ourselves, and after a few more days she learned to

perch on our ungloved hands without sinking her long talons in our flesh. She looked forward to our visits to break the monotony of her existence and came to enjoy her excursions to the living room to be shown off to visitors. She let anyone stroke her head and hold her with bare hands. I wondered if she understood and appreciated it when Athos said, "I am crazy about hawks. They are so intelligent."

After three weeks Athos took off her bonds to allow her to use her wings to flap about the bathroom. After a couple of days he set a post into the ground on the front terrace, put jesses on her legs, and attached her with a chain to the post. Quickly she learned that she could fly just so far—to the brick wall—and no farther. She liked her exercise that first day, and when dusk came she kept trying to fly to the house. Athos took her upon his hand and she rode docilely into her bathroom for the night, where she knew she was safe from harm.

After a few days of the hawk being outdoors during the day and brought into the house at night, Athos tried an experiment: after he untied her from the post he dropped the chain to the ground beside her. She walked directly to the front door, waited for him to open it, and entered the house. Would she know what to do next? She turned left to go into the bunkroom alone; there she turned right to go into the bathroom, and in the bathroom she hopped over the floor sill into the shower enclosure. She knew as well as we did where her bed was! Patiently she waited for Athos to come take off the chain for the night, and after that was done she promptly went to sleep. Every night thereafter she repeated the performance.

How nice that she liked our home! "Our home?" Why, it was hers just as much as it was ours, for she helped pay for it by posing for the pictures Athos painted of her. She owned us just as much as we owned her.

Daily we watched her exercising or in repose, and were sorry to observe that the broken wing,

Bald Eagle

though the bones had knitted, drooped somewhat. We hoped that in flying exercises this would be corrected, and the next step was to place her in the large aviary, where she could use her wings fully.

She could fly well enough to enjoy herself in the aviary, but in the months that followed we saw that she could not fly sufficiently well to be set free in the wild to look after herself. She was destined to live out her life span with the Menabonis; destined to give us a constant reminder of the gunman who had shot her; destined to make me ask people to please, please not shoot red-tailed hawks.

A year—two years—in confinement. She did not appear unhappy, yet I wondered what her thoughts were when high in the sky she could see other hawks of her kind in their element, free to go where they chose, to mate, and to live normally. I hoped that it was some compensation to know that her food would come every morning, from Athos's hands. Then, too, she was not alone, for in the next partition in the aviary was the Sergeant, not too different from her kind.

There she was, a perfectly healthy bird with a drooping wing. One morning Athos said to me, "I'm going to release her, to see if she can fly. After all, we could be mistaken; if we are, she ought to have her freedom." It was a gamble, but Athos wanted to risk it for her sake.

After being taken from the aviary, she slowly flapped her wings to gain a perch on a pine close by. For half a day she stayed there, looking about her familiar territory from a different vantage point. Then she opened each wing its full spread of sixteen inches, and flew off. She *could* fly well!

We wondered if we should ever see her again. Days passed, and once high in the sky we saw what appeared to be a red-tailed hawk soaring above Valle Ombrosa, but at that distance we could not determine if it was our pet or not. But a strange sound came from our aviary. After years of silence the Sergeant had let out a peculiar call, not a bit like the sound we had imagined a golden eagle to make, but like a small dog barking. Could it be that he recognized his former aviary mate? Was he calling to her?

A week went by, and one morning we heard a great commotion of chickens clattering alarm, ducks quacking, and pigeons flying. We rushed outside to see what was the cause, and there on a pine branch directly over the aviary sat our red-tailed hawk! The Sergeant was barking at her!

Athos looked at her and said, "Her crop is flat, she must be hungry. Perhaps she cannot fly well enough to catch her own food, and has come home for a handout." He rushed to get meat from the refrigerator.

Under the pine he stood with the meat on his outstretched hand. He called up to her, "Come on down. Here is your breakfast."

She opened her wings, dived downward, and glided to his feet. She walked a couple of steps to him and took the proffered piece of meat from his hands. After she had eaten it, she cried in a soft pitiful voice for more. Athos handed her another piece and another, until her crop bulged. When satisfied, she sprang into the air, and flew to a near-by tree, where she sat for hours. Then we saw a most peculiar thing happen. She flew onto the wire top of the eagle cage and stayed there. The Sergeant, in his cramped space, jumped off his perch, flipped himself upside down, and through the wire locked claws with the hawk! For five minutes the Sarge hung upside down in that clasp with her. She must have liked it, for after he turned her loose, and righted himself to go back to his perch, she waited on the wire for him to return to go through the same antic ten minutes later. Were they in love with each other? Was the Sergeant only playing?

With a loud, eerie, and weird scream she flew off. It was the kind of scream we should have expected to come from the eagle, but he only barked like a puppy as she left.

All right, she had come home, but a problem presented itself: would the hawk catch our other free birds? We soon found out that our fears were groundless, for the next morning she came back for breakfast. Every morning thereafter she returned, without once molesting the pigeons, ducks, or chickens. Why should she, when Athos is such a good provider?

And we always know by the barking of the Sergeant when she has arrived. Time after time we have seen them lock claws.

At the moment I see Athos on the hill by the hawk's favorite pine, and she is looking down at the rabbit in his hand, which he secured for her yesterday. I hear him saying, "Come on down. I can't stay here all day waiting for you to make up your mind! Come now."

And now she flies to his feet. The hawk of Valle Ombrosa is having her breakfast. She is so tame that, as she eats, I see Athos scratching the back of her head.

I remember the time when my father told Athos a story of his youth, when he went to live in Texas awhile. One day he and another man were riding on their horses talking of deer, and the man said that whenever he shot them he aimed at the heart. My father had never been deer hunting, but he said that if he did he would aim at the head. As they were discussing which would be the best method of killing a deer the quickest way, in the distance from among thick undergrowth rose a buck. As a generous gesture, the man told my father that he could have his first chance at securing a deer. Father aimed at the head and pulled the trigger. The buck fell.

The buck rose and started off. Again father aimed at the head and shot. The buck went down, this time not rising again. The men rode to the spot.

On the ground, within a couple of feet of each other, were *two* bucks, shot between the eyes! Then my father said, "Athos, when I looked at

their beautiful eyes, I made the decision that never again would I shoot anything for pleasure. Upon occasions of necessity I have hunted for food or to protect myself or my livestock, but right there in my teens I found that I could not kill creatures without a very good reason to do so. Have you ever looked into a deer's eyes?"

Athos had. Athos cannot go hunting deer.

Shortly after we moved to the rented country place, I wrote to my father about how we surprised a red fox drinking at the brook where the roar of the waterfall prevented him from hearing us or the wind had not blown our human odor toward him. Finally he spied us and ran some distance up the hill before sitting on his haunches for a long time observing us as we observed him. Many times thereafter we saw him. I must have asked father in that letter whether the fox would prey upon our birds, and also did he think the fox would be a menace with rabies?

I kept his reply, and I shall quote the letter exactly as it is:

Dear Sara and Athos:

To catch a fox you first put out some wood ashes thinly in a trail where you think a fox is likely to travel. Put some bait in two or three places so that when he eats it you will see his tracks and know that it is a fox. If he comes he will get the bait (fried sausage or meat scraps) but he may reach over from the side of the trail so as not to step in the ashes.

The ashes should be put where there is a tree or sapling to fasten a trap to. Then put out more ashes in the same place quite thick (an inch) and set your trap, fastening it very securely to the tree by means of the spike at the end of the chain. Put your trap in the middle of the ashes, cover it thinly with ashes so that no part of it can be seen. Put bait on both sides of the trap (not on the trap), so that when Mr. Fox eats on one side he may take another step to get the other bait and possibly put his foot in it. He does not like the human smell and is very likely smarter than you, getting the bait without getting caught.

You have to visit your traps early every morning. He may get caught but he will pull the chain loose if possible, or even chew off his foot. It is interesting to pit your human wisdom against a fox's cunning.

Your father has done it.

I didn't doubt it a bit, and I was interested to hear of something else that he had done in his youth. But I wrote back to him that I'd bet a nickel that at present he would not set out any fox traps, but would enjoy seeing foxes in the wild as we did. Athos and I had no intention of trying to trap the fox, but thanks just the same for telling us how it was done.

Athos and I have had a great many birds of prey, and during the meat shortage our friends did their utmost to provide us with whatever meat they could find. One time a friend telephoned that red foxes were killing his poultry; he had trapped a baby fox and did we want it to feed the eagle and hawk? We said yes, of course.

We had presumed that it was dead, but when he arrived with the box, we saw that the fox was living. After the man left, I said, "Athos, if you are going to kill it, do it quickly—and while I am not looking."

"I can't kill it," he said.

Naturally he could not kill the poor little frightened creature. He had the appearance of a puppy, an adorable puppy; but Athos was not deluded by his appearance. He used his heavy leather gloves when putting a leather collar around his neck, attached a chain to the collar, and securely attached the chain to a stake outside our bunkroom window. Athos built a little house for him. And we had another mouth to feed! Where could we get enough meat? We should have to bait our friends into taking a greater interest in our critters and catching our enthusiasm over this new addition to Valle Ombrosa. Food would come from *somewhere:* it always did.

Within a week, Foxy was eating from our hands, but he was highly nervous and we had to approach him exactly to his liking or he would scoot into his house. In time we took him walking, keeping a firm grasp on the chain, and he liked that very much. Came the day of major achievement when he jumped up on a low brick wall, stretched out to take a sun bath, and, after our showing him our intention very slowly, suffered us to stroke his fur and scratch his body.

Everyone tells us that we may *think* we can tame a fox, but when he is adult he may at any moment become vicious. A solicitous lawyer friend has given Athos a lecture, asking if his hands are insured against injury? Foxy must smell the odor of fear from these persons, for when they approach him he is scared and scampers into his house for safety. Of course we appreciate the concern and warnings of our friends, but they forget that we have had tutelage from both of our fathers as to what to do in emergencies. The foremost rule is: do not be terrified.

What will happen when Foxy is fully grown? That will be taken care of when the time comes. At present we are enjoying him. As I look out my window now, I see that he is enjoying living. To amuse him Athos gave Foxy an emptied coconut shell to play with. He is like a puppy with his toy, leaping and turning somersaults, rolling the shell, nudging it, then jumping away. When the toy is out of reach of his chain length, he becomes sad. Right now I must go outdoors and give his toy back to him.

CHAPTER ELEVEN

THIS MORNING Athos had been outdoors while I prepared breakfast. On entering the house he said, "If I were God, which I'm not, and if I could create a perfect day, which I can't, this would be the masterpiece."

I glanced out of the window, then spoke of the mountainous duties that would shut out the sunshine of living for me this morning; in the shadow of the house I would work at housekeeping; on my desk was a tremendous pile of letters that had to be answered—oh, there were hundreds of responsibilities and duties to claim my entire time. I told Athos that I was sorry but I simply could not go outdoors.

Athos has a good memory. He picked up the book I had left lying open last night and read aloud to me what Longfellow had written: " 'If Spring came but once in a century instead of once a year, or burst forth with the sound of an earthquake and not in silence, what wonder and expectation there would be in all hearts to behold the miraculous change.' "

"I know, Athos; that is a beautiful thought, beautifully presented. I wish that I could write that way. Oh, I have so much to learn about writing! I'm still in the state of putting too many hyphens in compound words and I don't know how to write a—"

I was startled by the loud noise of Athos slamming shut the book. I was annoyed that he had lost the page where I had left off reading. Then I saw the expression on his face and I wondered what was coming next from him.

"Sara, how many more springtimes will you have in your life? If you are lucky, there will be thirty or so. Maybe there will be only twenty—something could happen to you so that there would be only ten more springtimes for you."

I nearly broke down the door getting out.

It *was* a masterpiece of a day, and how very nearly I had come to missing it all! "Oh, Athos, thank you for rescuing me! Look! the Siberian iris and lilies by the wall are coming up. The redbud trees and dogwoods are full of buds about to burst open. Will the crabapple trees bloom this year for the first time? Oh, Athos, the great masses of yellow blooms of January jasmine and jonquils!"

Down the driveway, we stopped to see two bluebirds investigate a birdhouse on a post. Time and again they flew to the hole to peer inside, "standing still" in mid-air, with only a flutter of wings. We left them considering that possible nesting site.

Will the white and lavender wisterias, which have climbed up pines, bloom this year for the first time? The climbing roses were doing well on the railing by the driveway. We exclaimed over the "riot of green" of the bush honeysuckle along the road, and over the greenery surrounding the gate. Why had we worked to plant all these things if not to enjoy them when they were finally putting on a show for us? I thought of all the magnificent estates near by, where we never saw the owners outdoors looking at the beauties that had been brought to perfection by their gardeners. Were those estates merely theatrical settings, waiting, waiting endlessly for living persons to come on-stage? Athos and I had made our little stage ourselves and were upon it. By the grace of God we were *living* on every inch of our ground!

We turned our backs to the gate to go into the valley proper. We paused to watch a towhee busily scratching among the leaves under bushes. The planted bamboo was helping to make this area thicker for nesting sites, shelter, and escape from enemies.

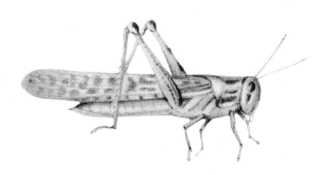

Ah, the thicket. And sadness entered into my joy as I remembered last Sunday morning when we had decided to go outside our gate, across the road, to walk in acres we did not own. We had gone into the wilderness that had a beautiful creek meandering through it: a place that the birds loved with a passion. As we strolled farther down the creek (beyond the boundary line of the land our friend owned, the one who had told us to enjoy those acres) we received a sudden shock. True, we had seen the big sign that had been put up by a real estate firm offering those acres for sale at an enormous price, but we had not known that a gang of workmen had been sent to "beautify" the property. It was all bare, except for trees here and there. The superb canebrake was gone, every bush and shrub on the banks of the creek was cut down—all the handsome pink honeysuckle, the wild plum trees, the cherries, and horse sugar, and dogwoods, and ferns, and Heaven only knows what else that Athos and I had looked upon a hundred times, marveling. Bare ground, bare creekbanks. We declared that to us the acres were not worth ten cents now.

But we had gone on in that devastated area and saw—oh, I hate to tell this—that the huge silver-bell tree that we had discovered there last spring, with its thousands of small white bell-shaped blooms, had been cut down. One of the most breath-takingly lovely trees when in bloom, gone; a few minutes' work with an ax had

destroyed that magnificent life. Had no one cared that the silver-bell was one of the rare trees in his area? Surely he must not have known that it was a specimen tree to be saved at all cost, but in ignorance had cut it up and carted it away to some dump heap. Athos and I would have given our entire bank account for that one tree, and then would have felt that we had bought it cheap.

Since we were suffering with each step, I do not know why we continued to go on over that land. Good God in Heaven, why? WHY? To make a rough footbridge across the creek a tremendous sycamore had been felled, solely for the convenience of the workmen. That marvelous sycamore had lived a hundred or two hundred years in glory, to be destined to die so that the dirty shoes of hired men should walk over the trunk!

It was too much for us; Athos and I became so sick emotionally that we became physically ill. We fled back to the sanctuary of Valle Ombrosa. As we returned through our gate, Athos said, "No one can touch all this that is ours! 'Ours'? In truth, it is not ours—we are only the *custodians* of these trees for a short time. We have it only an infinitesimal time in the limitless time of the universe."

And so today, as I passed slowly alongside the thicket, I was glad that the birds, who had for innumerable generations returned spring after spring to their habitual nesting area, could move from diagonally across the road into the sanctuary that we have designated for birds. Suppose we had cut out our canebrake, cleared away our tangled thicket—what could the birds have done this spring?

We walked alongside the brook, our Lys, so different from the one in the Alps. Our Lys was bordered with dogwoods, violets, and the dried stalks of last year's flowers that indicated to us where a new crop of plants would again grow to delight our senses. We saw our umbrella trees with big leaf buds—trees, trees, trees, all working violently on such a spring day to swell their leaf buds.

We went to the little lake, named Larghetto Jenny, in honor of Athos's mother, and already planted, so that in time the flora will obliterate the newness and it will appear as a natural lake. The living Christmas present—the wood ducks— was giving us delight every day of the year. The ducks' reflections mirrored in the placid water gave us two more birds! Will they nest in the house Athos has made for them at the edge of the water? Or will they find a convenient tree hole somewhere on our hill?

The Canada geese came to eat bread out of our hands. Oh, yes, Athos had had foresight enough to bring the food for them.

The mallards were busy diving, and there is nothing I had rather see than upended ducks with their amusing little curled tail feathers. On the hillsides were brush heaps that someone might think were trash piles, but they were there for a purpose; already under each heap is a mallard nest with an egg or two or three. What sights are in store for us when one by one the mallard mothers will lead their downy babies to the water for their first swims! No more bathtubs for our ducklings.

The planted winged elms are living, so are the fringe trees, and so are the little sycamores. Maybe we shall never see these sycamores towering tall and magnificent, but someone will when we are dead and gone. That is, if some future owner of Valle Ombrosa does not cut them down!

On we went to the Azalea Pool, which spills with two waterfalls into Larghetto Jenny. The native azaleas surrounding the pool have buds that before long will be dreamlike pink and orange and flame masses of blooms. We sat for a while upon the huge slab of granite that nature placed beside the pool and looked up into the branches of the beech, which still holds a couple of last year's birds' nests. In a crevice of the roots of the beech a hepatica was in bloom.

We crossed the brook to go up the hillside where once we had had a terraced Victory Garden, which for two seasons had proved to be our "defeat garden" despite our hard work. But victory we had determined to have in a different way. On the same plot of ground, instead of growing vegetables, we have planted grapes and fruit trees, and they are thriving nicely. Should we never have fruit from the trees, we hope to feast our eyes on the blossoms of pear, peach, cherry, and plum trees.

I thought of the words of Bryant:

Ye have no history. I ask in vain
Who planted on the slope this lofty group
Of ancient pear trees, that with springtime burst
Into such breadth of bloom. One bears a scar
Where the quick lightning scored its trunk, yet still
It feels the breath of spring, and every May
Is white with blossoms. Who it was that laid
Their infant roots in earth, and tenderly
Cherished the delicate sprays, I ask in vain,
Yet bless the unknown hand to which I owe
This annual festival of bees, these songs
Of birds within their leafy screens, these shouts
Of joy from children gathering up the fruit
Shaken in August from the willing boughs.

Back along the valley we walked, this time beside the curving rock wall that outlines the foot of the hill. It was the first project Athos had

undertaken when first we bought the land, and I remembered his picking up every rock, placing every one—and today it is a finished project, with ivy upon it, lilies and foamflowers coming up beside it. A wall that appears to have been there for ages, yet made only a few years ago.

But the drift of leaves had piled so high beside one side of the wall that they were covering the moss on the ground. We had to help the moss. We fetched a bamboo rake and a box, and went to work raking away those dead leaves that were killing the moss underneath. We carted away the leaves in the big box to the wheelbarrow, and wheeled them away. Oh, not to burn them, for we know better than to burn leaves; they were dumped where they would do good, by rotting and fertilizing ground that needed this assistance.

After we had finished with our work we ambled past my rock garden. That little area which had been my first project was now a finished one. The flora that I had personally planted was bursting with spring-gladness—the trumpet honeysuckle vines were putting out new leaves, the wild roses had leaf buds, the foamflowers had tiny leaves, the violets were coming up and so were the trilliums. Forgotten now were my past backaches, broken fingernails, perspiration, and the frustration I had felt.

Then we climbed up the long flight of stone steps that Athos and Ike have labored on for years. Labored? That word is inappropriate, for each time Ike had placed a stone at Athos's direction, Ike had said proudly, "That rock will be there when I am dead and gone," and found comfort in the thought of the legacy of beauty he will leave behind. Each time a step was placed, Athos found pleasure in erasing the newness by tucking moss between the crevices, and on each side planting irises, lilies, jonquils, hepatica, ferns, verbena, sedum, wild strawberries, and many other plants. Physical labor, yes, but a labor to achieve beauty.

At the top of the steps we stopped to look at the feeding station for the birds (as if we do not daily see it from our window!), for we had to admire at close range the trumpet flower and trumpet honeysuckle twined about the post. On the house is trumpet vine. (We certainly went in for trumpets!) Near by is the hedge of abelia bushes, for the aesthetic value, yes, but more than that: the ruby-throated hummingbirds like to feed on all these flowers.

We were reluctant to enter the house. Athos teased me by saying that I did not want to go inside to all the dishes that awaited me in the kitchen sink! Oh, no, the dishes would not walk away, but I could walk to the belvedere to see how the flora was thriving there and to enjoy the view of the valley. Not just *our* valley. My thoughts were crowded with remembrances of dozens of supper parties there under the stars, and the hundreds of Sunday afternoon visitors who had sat there sipping welcome cold drinks after their "tours of inspection" of Valle Ombrosa. How very, very gratifying that all this had not been ours alone. How much pleasure I can anticipate for the future as that belvedere will hold countless others who shall, with us, survey the shady valley. Today, scattered at great distances over this nation—even in foreign lands—are people, now unknown to us, who will some-day be chatting with us on our belvedere.

At long last I returned to the house, thinking, if I were God, and if I had created a perfect spring day, the least I should expect of people to whom I had given so lavishly would be that they should avail themselves of this loveliness.

Yesterday Athos and I stood in our sanctuary, saying confidently: "No one can touch all this that is ours. We have paid good money for our acres, we have paper deeds and titles to our land, we have worked hard upon it to save its natural beauty and improve it. We have made it into a haven for wildlife, a sanctuary providing peace and serenity and security for ourselves, and to offer sanctuary to hundreds of visitors annually,

Mourning Dove

and, by proxy, to thousands of others who may never come to Valle Ombrosa but who have learned about the place and feel it in their hearts as one paradise on earth. We are fully aware that we are guardians of the land and all its God-given contents." Smugly we had said that no one could harm it.

But today I quake with fear and tremble with dread over the unknown factor—what other people will do. And I am burning with anger, hot with the outrage perpetrated against us. Pent-up emotions boil within me as I ask: Is there no security anywhere at all? One person with fire in his hands, whether by intent or through negligence, can be a criminal in starting a forest fire. I who have done nothing to deserve such treatment am unarmed to defend myself.

Yesterday afternoon my husband and I left Valle Ombrosa, to go to a concert with some friends, and afterwards went to the home of other friends for the evening. A perfect end to a beautiful day. All was well in our world. Drowsily we drove homeward.

As we turned from the main highway into our little country road, I was startled by Athos: "Look! A burning stump in the woods!"

By the automobile headlights we saw that alongside the road the ground had been burned —since we had left in midafternoon. God only knew how the fire had been started, but He had not done it with lightning nor was it a case of spontaneous combustion. We saw that the fire was out, and only here and there was some rotting wood still smoldering.

My heart stood still as we continued on to our gate. Had all of Valle Ombrosa gone up in flames while we had been at the concert and the home of our friends? Had the eagle, owl, and other birds been trapped in the aviary as in a fiery furnace? Yama, Charlotte, the grosbeak, and the dove had been locked inside the house! Were the trees seared; had the bushes and little plants vanished in smoky air? Had the Menabonis'

dream, which had become a reality, entirely gone up in smoke? Were only ruins left? I was frantic in the grip of fear.

Ah, the gate was intact. But I could not see the huge glass windows of the tiny house. If it was burned, not all the insurance money in the world could replace it. None of its contents could be replaced—not just the furnishings, but the pictures that had flowed from Athos's heart, and even my own manuscript. Worst of all, had Yama perished, our faithful, devoted, trusting dog, who had once survived the bite of a poisonous snake; our dear little Charlotte, who had miraculously overcome her almost total paralysis; our rose-breasted grosbeak, who had been saved from untimely death by a gun bullet—were they dead, dead, dead? It was an interminable time before Athos got the automobile inside the gateway, to proceed up the hill. I prayed—prayed—

At last the light from the automobile shone upon the glass windows: the house stood, and I could breathe again. The aviary was dimly outlined, and I could sigh with relief. There were no signs of fire on our land.

Athos no sooner entered the house than he left it again with his flashlight, to examine the ground beside the wire fence that enclosed our acres. He reported that someone had been inside Valle Ombrosa, had raked a "firebreak" and thus kept the fire from entering our property. I telephoned to the nearest fire department to ask information, and was told that someone had telephoned to summon the firemen to put out the fire for us. (There is not a telephone within a quarter of a mile of us. Had some neighbor seen the smoke and come to investigate? Had some passing motorist put in the call to the fire department?)

Last night we had thought that all the devastation had stopped at the fence, but this morning Athos discovered that the flames had come inside at the top of the hill. Had the firemen not come at the exact moment they did, the fire would have got the aviary. It had been stopped two feet from the wooden structure.

Athos has read the signs. He knows from whence the fire came. He knows that the firemen checked the fire by raking a clear space on the ground. He knows by the tire marks that the fire truck came up the driveway to the house (and what a fright Yama must have had in the house!) and the driver must have had a dickens of a time turning the big truck around. He knows that the truck was too wide for the confines of the driveway made for ordinary automobiles, for the truck knocked down the rock dry-walls that outlined the driveway. Rock by rock, backache by backache, those walls must be rebuilt. But what unlimited gratitude we have for those firemen.

One woods fire making me all hot and bothered? No, this is the fourth fire in the woods about Valle Ombrosa. Twice, oddly enough each time on Easter Sunday afternoon, Athos and I had labored alone to extinguish fires caused perhaps by a cigarette thrown from an automobile, or a pile of raked leaves or trash left to burn unattended, or by a fire set to "clear" a woods. While others were enjoying their Easters, we had been working like mad.

One fire had been so bad that our neighbors, who had not previously met us, of their own accord and out of sympathy came to our help. But even their exertions were insufficient, and we summoned the fire department. I shall never forget that inferno, the overfatigue that I experienced, and how I finally collapsed on the ground, gasping for breath.

Some persons, unknown to me, have certainly tried their level best for the fourth time to burn Valle Ombrosa. But this morning it remains an oasis of greenery and life, whereas on the other side of the fence the earth is black, the trees are scorched, and the smell of the smoke from smoldering logs is disagreeable to the nostrils.

It is unjust that I should have to harbor fears that someday I may return to find my home, my land, my creatures, my bit of nature, entrusted to me as custodian, destroyed. My sanctuary—a holy place—is not secure. The sanctity should be inviolable, but it isn't. I have had demonstrated to me that security is only an illusion, for some people have arson in their hearts, whether from lack of intelligence, from carelessness, or from intent to hurt others.

We do not have children to inherit Valle Ombrosa. When we are no longer custodians of it, someone—no matter who—will come into possession of it; and we hope that we may pass it on as a legacy to be enjoyed as we today are enjoying it. But I see that we have to fight for what we intend to pass on to our heirs.

Brown Thrasher

CHAPTER TWELVE

*T*HIS MORNING leaf buds were bursting open everywhere, creating a riot of greens. With his artist's eye, which takes in complex colors in all their hues and tints, Athos has taught me to see all of the variations of greens that I may appreciate their subtlety as much as I do the more obvious colors of autumn. No longer am I content with the one word "green." This morning I saw a humble, lowly thistle coming up; that is a "green" plant. Green, yes, but on top there was bluish-green, and beneath the lobed, ruffled, prickly leaves was whitish-green, and the curled and twisted many-lobed leaves were edged with a purple line. The green plant had woolly hairs all over, which glistened silver in the sunlight. Multiply this observation I made of a single plant, and consider all the greens that Athos sees outdoors. People speak of him as a "born artist," yet he was not born with skilled eyes. He has trained his eyes to see the minute details that he later paints, and he has been trying to train my eyes. There are, of course, people who think that we spend hours outdoors merely "playing."

My conscience bothered me not at all that I was "wasting" a perfectly good morning. I stopped to examine the new leaves of the blue (or pagoda) dogwood, to poke under dead leaves to see if fern fronds were coming up, seeing the bronzy-red opened cluster of leaves of the dwarf buckeye, observing my hillside dotted with white bloodroot blossoms and delicate, pinkish-white rue anemones, and a few purple and white violets already in bloom, and wild plum blossoms, slightly fragrant. There was emerald moss, springy underfoot. I was getting

what I needed personally. How I should later apply to some good purpose what I personally achieved was something I did not bother about at the moment.

Oho! Who is this? The first brown thrasher of the season at Valle Ombrosa. "Welcome home! Maybe Athos will paint another picture of you," I said. The thrasher, however, did not seem to be impressed. He was not paying any attention to my talking; he was "frozen." That immobility told *me* things.

I looked into the sky, to see a Cooper's hawk circling overhead. The villain was on the stage with a backdrop of blue sky and wisps of white clouds. Then another actor came into the drama —a sparrow hawk after the Cooper's hawk, screaming "killy-killy-killy." Despite the fact that the sparrow hawk was much smaller, he was fighting mad at the intrusion of the other hawk into *his* territory.

They went on their way and I went on my way. I had not gone far before I witnessed three Carolina black-capped chickadees having a battle royal. Tsch, tsch, on such a pretty morning fighting each other! Was it a case of the eternal triangle, and who should get the most desirable female? Or were they squabbling over who should possess Valle Ombrosa for a house site?

The columbines were coming up. I remembered the man who had visited us and had seen us nursing our two columbines. He said that he would write to his mother in another state to collect some of her columbine seeds for us. Although she did not know us, she had sent a box of seeds with directions as to how to plant them. She did not get my thank-you letter, for she died suddenly. Or is she dead? A part of her will live indefinitely, for her columbines will bloom year after year and re-seed the ground.

I saw a squirrel scampering up a tree. Wistfully I remembered our Sussi and Biribissi. When they were old enough we released them outdoors, and every night they returned to sleep in our house on their favorite closet shelf on top of Athos's shirts. But alas, predators or gunmen outside our fence took the lives of our pets, so that we have no tangible reminders of them save the gnawed buttons on Athos's shirts. Could the squirrel I saw this morning be a female and will she have some babies this year to enliven Valle Ombrosa anew?

Yama "jumped" a rabbit—the two were off in a flash of bounding legs. I called the dog, not that I expected or feared that he would catch the rabbit in the chase; he is a smart one, that rabbit, and each time knows to run straight for the gate to escape through the wooden bars that Yama cannot squeeze through. For four years that rabbit has been successful in eluding Yama. This morning I had seen that the rabbit had eaten a new shoot of a Cherokee rose, but that was all right with me: it is his sanctuary, too. Yama returned to me, knowing that I considered his escapade "wrong," for he came slinking with his tail between his legs. I gave him a good scolding about chasing the bunny, and he all but said, "You know good and well that we were just having a good run," and I had to forgive him, or rather, he forgave me for having the wrong thoughts about his intentions. His tail wagged

again. Yama has never caught a living thing; has never eaten a living thing.

I jumped a big frog in my path, but he never moved a muscle or altered his stare. Why didn't he leap into the brook two feet distant? Does a frog get sick? When I returned by the same path, again I played leapfrog.

The murmur of my brook—not the roar of the Lys in the Alps—the sigh of the wind in my pines, the bluebirds singing "Purity, Purity," the Carolina wrens singing and whirring, the "dee-dee-dee" of a chickadee, the unmistakable call of a flicker in the distance, the tapping of a red-headed woodpecker against a tree trunk, the sequent notes "quank-quank-quank" of the white-breasted nuthatch, the "pe-tow, pe-tow" of the tufted titmouse, all formed a symphonic accompaniment to the vigorous carol of a robin who carried the melody of the "Spring Song."

I joined Athos by the lake. It is a bit early to be finding Easter eggs, but Athos had found two pale-green eggs on the bank of Larghetto Jenny, laid by our well-fed mallards, who often drop their eggs just any old place instead of in their nests.

But I do not have to be reminded today that spring is officially here; everything in nature pro-

claims it. This morning we went to our garden, to plant still more seeds although we had vowed to have only a tiny vegetable garden this year. While we worked, Athos sang an Italian folk song in counterpart to my singing "The Red Old Hills of Georgia." And the Canada geese came to stand by the side of the fence, softly honking.

Some little animal had cropped our strawberry plants to the roots. Never mind, the creature must have something to eat, and he innocently thought the strawberries had been planted there for him by a generous nature. We also found something to eat that nature offered to us gratis: poke greens for lunch.

This minute I see that my husband is using his hands to paint a bird picture. It is the product of the seed of love for birds planted in his childhood in Italy.

Green-winged Teal

DESCRIPTIONS FOR COLOR PLATES

HOODED MERGANSER

(*Lophodytes cucullatus*)

Length—sixteen to nineteen inches. The male hooded merganser is a strikingly marked black and white bird, with cinnamon-rufous sides finely marked with black and a conspicuous fan-shaped black and white crest. The dark female has a reddish-brown crest and a white speculum. Mergansers can be distinguished from other ducks by their long, slender, serrate bills. These diving ducks, which mainly inhabit fresh water and are tree nesters, can be found in timberland over the northern part of the continent wherever there are quiet ponds and streams. The nest is in a tree cavity or hollow stump and may contain from six to eighteen white eggs. Page ix

BLUE JAY

(Cyanocitta cristata)

Length—eleven to twelve inches. The sexes are alike in color. This large bird, with its crested head and bright blue wings and tail, is easily identifiable. It is found in eastern North America to the Great Plains, and south to central Florida. It has a variety of notes, some musical, some imitative, as well as the harsh, slurring *jay!* for which it is well known. It is omnivorous, but prefers mast. Nesting in trees, preferably evergreen, the female lays from three to six eggs variable in color from buff to greenish with varying shades of brown spots. Page xii

BOBOLINK

(*Dolichonyx oryzivorus*)

Length—six and one-half to eight inches. The male in spring breeding plumage is the only songbird that is black below with white patches above; the back of the head is yellowish cream. Females, young birds, and males in winter plumage are a yellowish buff with dark stripes on the head and underparts. They are known as "reedbirds" or "ricebirds." The song is a bubbling melody, given on the wing, but when migrating in flocks they have a call note that is a metallic *chink*. Bobolinks feed on grain, seeds, insects, and fruit. They breed from Cape Breton Island, southern Ontario, southern Manitoba, and southeastern British Columbia south to New Jersey, Pennsylvania, Colorado, and northeastern California, and winter in southern South America. The nest is made of grasses and is placed in a slight depression in the ground. It may contain from five to seven grayish-white to reddish-brown eggs marked with splotches and spots of brown and purple. Page xvi

CARDINAL

(*Cardinalis cardinalis*)

Length—Eight and one-quarter inches. The male is distinguished from other red birds by its crest, conical red bill, and black mask extending to the throat. The female has a crest and dull red wings and tail, but is olive brown above and buff colored below. Cardinals can be found in the eastern United States from New England south to the Gulf States and west to the Great Plains, in almost every type of land habitat. Their song is a full, clear whistle, with variations, and a call note, *tsip!* They feed primarily on seeds, berries, and other vegetable matter, but eat some insects. A loosely constructed nest is made in thickets, saplings, or bushes, and may contain three or four bluish- or greenish-white eggs marked with varying shades of browns. There are two broods a year. Page 9

BARN SWALLOW

(*Hirundo rustica*)

Length—more or less seven inches. The field marks of the barn swallow are the deeply forked tail with some white, the chestnut-rufous forehead, throat, and upper breast, and the blue-black back. The females and young are paler. These birds have cheerful twittering voices, but their fame lies in their power and ease in flight. They feed almost exclusively on insects captured on the wing. Barn swallows breed over much of Canada and Alaska and south to North Carolina, Alabama, Arkansas, and central Mexico, and winter from Mexico to Argentina. In pairs or colonies they make nests of mud, bonded with grasses and lined with soft materials; they are plastered against vertical or horizontal surfaces, originally in caves and on cliffs, but now usually on man-made structures. The nests may contain four or five white eggs marked with reddish- or olive-brown, and two broods are raised each year. Page 13

LEAST TERN

(*Sterna antillarum*))

Length—eight and one-half to nine and one-half inches. The summer coloration of this very small tern is pearl gray, white, and touches of black, with yellow bill and feet. The voice is a shrill squeal. When looking for fish and crustaceans, it flies with the bill pointed downward. It breeds in small colonies on the Atlantic and Gulf coasts from Maine to the Florida Keys and the West Indies, on the Pacific coast to southern Mexico, and on inland river islands and sand bars. It winters from the Gulf Coast to Central America and Brazil. The nest is merely a slight depression in the sand and may contain from two to four buff eggs spotted with brown. Page 16

AMERICAN KESTREL

(*Falco sparverius*)

Length—nine to twelve inches. This slender, rufous-tailed falcon may be found from Canada to southern South America. Males have slate-blue wings, the females rufous-red wings; the underparts are spotted in males and streaked in females. Perched on telephone wires, fence posts, and dead trees, kestrels watch for grasshoppers and mice. After they see their prey they fly directly above it, a rapid beating of the wings enabling them to hover at quite a height before pouncing. Their call is a shrill *killy-killy-killy*. The kestrel is the only North American hawk that commonly nests in tree holes. The female lays from four to seven eggs, variable in color from cream to reddish buff, speckled with brown. Page 21

HOODED WARBLER

(*Wilsonia citrina*)

Length—five and one-half inches. The male is easily identified by his black hood, bright yellow face and forehead, and the flashing patches of white on the outer tail feathers. The female shows only a trace of black about her head. These insect-eating birds are found in damp woods and thickets throughout the eastern part of the United States and west to the edge of the Great Plains. They winter in Central America. They have a loud and pleasant song and a sharp call note, *tzip!* The compactly woven nest is generally made in bushes and may contain four or five white eggs speckled with brown. Page 25

PURPLE GALLINULE

(*Porphyrula martinica*)

Length—twelve to fourteen inches. This colorful bird is identifiable by its pale frontal shield on the forehead and its yellow legs. The purple gallinule has a variety of clucking calls and chick-enlike notes. Its food is mostly aquatic vegetation, but includes snails and insects, as well as seeds and berries. It breeds from Tennessee and Maryland south to Peru and northern Argentina, and winters from Florida and southern Texas southward. The nest is a platform built of reeds or rushes in grassy marshes or over water. It may contain from four to ten buff-white eggs speckled with brown. Page 33

AMERICAN ROBIN

(*Turdus migratorius*)

Length—eight and one-half to ten and one-half inches. The sexes are similar in color, but the female is paler. Young robins have speckled breasts. Robins, familiar to most people, are noted for their brick-red breasts and the blue-green color of their eggs. They belong to the thrush family. The voice has an extended range, the most recognizable call being the loud caroling in two-or three-note phrases. The diet includes worms, insects, fruit, and berries. The range of the robin is over most of North America from Alaska to Mexico, and from Newfoundland to the Gulf Coast. The nest, usually five to fifteen feet above the ground and most frequently built in fruit or shade trees (sometimes on a projection from a house or barn), is made of grasses, twigs, and rootlets, often interwoven with rags, twine, or paper. It has an inner wall of mud, finished with a lining of fine grasses and may contain from three to five greenish-blue eggs. Two broods, or sometimes three, are raised each year. Page 37

MALLARD

(*Anas platyrhynchos*)

Length—twenty to twenty-eight inches. The male is easily identifiable by his striking green head and neck. The female is very similar to the female black duck but paler, with a whitish tail and white borders on both sides of her speculum. The mallard is found in abundance over most of the Northern Hemisphere. This game bird inhabits ponds, rivers, and brackish waters. The female has a much louder *quack* than the male. Surface-feeders, mallards are almost entirely vegetarian. The nest is built on the ground and may contain from six to ten light buff-green eggs. Page 41

CAROLINA CHICKADEE

(*Parus carlinensis*)

Length—four and three-quarters inches or smaller. This southern relative of the black-capped chickadee has less white on the wings. It likes human offerings of peanut butter and suet to add to its diet of insects, larvae, seeds, fruits, and berries. The high-pitched call—*dee-dee-dee*—may become four syllables. In tree or stump holes and bird boxes, the nest is made of grasses, moss, feathers, and plant down, and may contain from five to ten white eggs speckled with brown. Resident farther south than the black-capped, the Carolina chickadee can be found from New Jersey, Louisiana, and Oklahoma to Florida, the Gulf Coast, and central Texas. Page 45

BOBWHITE

(*Colinus virginianus*)

Length—eight and one-half to ten and one-half inches. The bobwhite is a distinctly North American bird, which hunters often call a "quail." The adult male and female have about the same colors and markings, except that the male has a white throat and stripe over the eye, while in the female these are buff. In spring the male marks and claims his territory by whistling the loud *Bob-white!* At other seasons, when the birds are grouped in a covey, there is a scatter call, and the birds signal one another to come together with soft, sweet chirping notes. They roost on the ground tail to tail, with their heads pointing outward. They consume grains, insects, and berries. Bobwhites are found from Texas, the Gulf States, and Florida north to Maine and across the northern states to South Dakota. There is an isolated population in the Pacific Northwest. The nest is built on the ground and made of grasses; it may contain from ten to eighteen white eggs. Page 49

WILD TURKEY

(*Meleagris gallopavo*)

Length—male: forty-eight to fifty inches; female: thirty-six inches. Wild turkeys differ from domestic turkeys by having chestnut rather than white on the tail tips. Wild turkeys formerly had a greater range, but after being extirpated in many areas, they are being successfully reintroduced in many states. Usually traveling in small flocks, these birds inhabit woodlands where they can find mast, weed seeds, berries, buds, and some insects. Polygamists, gobblers have two or three hens. The female makes her well-hidden nest in a shallow depression in the ground, sparingly lined, and lays from eight to eighteen brown-speckled light-buff eggs. Page 52

BOAT-TAILED GRACKLE

(*Quiscalus major*)

Length—male: sixteen and one-half inches; female: twelve and one-half inches. The sooty-brown female is much smaller than her mate, and she lacks his magnificent iridescence. These grackles are found near salt water from New Jersey to the Gulf States, the Florida Keys, and southeastern Texas. Their calls are a mixture of whistles, clucks, and squeaks. They eat crustaceans, mollusks, insects, and grains and breed in loose colonies in marshes and swamps. These grackles coat the inside of their nests with mud and the female lays three or four pale blue eggs, spotted, blotched, and scrawled with browns and purple. Page 57

CANADA GOOSE

(*Branta canadensis*)

Length—twenty-five to forth-three inches. The sexes are alike in color, but the male is slightly larger than the female. Fast-flying Canada geese, with a wingspread of five to six and one-half feet, are common over most of North America. More adapted to land than ducks, they can be found away from water, grazing on herbage, in grain fields, and even on lawns and golf courses, since their food is mainly vegetable. While flying or on water they trumpet, *hoonck*, but when feeding they utter a number of soft, intimate notes. Mating for life, a pair selects a nesting site on the ground near water. The nest is made of twigs and grasses and lined with down and may contain from four to ten dull white eggs. Canada geese may live for fifty years or more. Page 65

PILEATED WOODPECKER

(*Dryocopus pileatus*)

Length—seventeen and one-half inches. The sexes are similar in coloring, but the female has red only on her crest. Pileated woodpeckers are found in the wooded regions of North America, mainly east of the Rocky Mountains. They are noted for their large size, their prominent black and white coloration, and their conspicuous red crest. The voice resembles that of a flicker, but these woodpeckers make a louder and deeper series of *kuks*. The "song," made by beating the bill against a hard surface, is a long, hollow drumming. The diet includes ants, grubs, beetles, wild fruits, and berries. These woodpeckers nest in a cavity in a dead tree or tall stump, and lay from three to six white eggs. Page 69

NORTHERN FLICKER

(*Colaptes auratus*)

Length—thirteen to fourteen inches. Flickers are the only large brownish woodpeckers in North America. The eastern form, known also as the yellow-shafted flicker, has bright yellow under the wings and in the tail, and in flight shows a conspicuous white rump. The male has a black stripe on each side of the throat. Flickers often feed on the ground; ants are the most important food, but a variety of other insects and berries are also eaten. In addition to its loud ringing call, the flicker also drums on hollow limbs or roofs, making a long, rolling noise that proclaims its nesting territory. The yellow-striped flicker breeds in Canada east of the Rockies and to the limit of trees in Alaska, south to southern Florida and the Gulf Coast. It winters from Maine, the Great Lakes, and South Dakota to the Gulf Coast and Texas. The nest is in a cavity, preferably in a tall dead tree. From six to eight white eggs form the usual clutch. Page 117

BELTED KINGFISHER

(*Ceryle alcyon*)

Length—eleven to fourteen inches. The belted kingfisher is one of the few species where the female is brighter in color than the male. She has a russet band, which the male lacks, across and down the sides of the belly. Kingfishers have an unmistakable loud rattling call. They breed from Alaska, Manitoba, and Labrador to California and the Gulf of Mexico, wintering from British Columbia, Illinois, Ohio, and southern New England south to Central and South America. They are fish eaters and are rarely found far from water. The nest is laid in a long tunnel in a bank and may contain from five to eight white eggs. Page 124

SNOWY EGRET

(*Egretta thula*)

Length—twenty-four to twenty-seven inches. Noted for its exquisite nuptial plumes, this white bird has yellow feet, black legs, and a black bill that is yellow at the base and on lores. Generally silent, snowy egrets can give an hoarse croak or hiss. They feed on aquatic life, favoring marshes, salt bays, ponds, and beaches. In late summer it may be seen in New England and the Great Lakes, but it winters only as far north as California and South Carolina It breeds in the warmer parts of the United States, south to Chile and northern Argentina. In colonies with other herons and ibises, near or over water in low trees or bushes, the snowy egret constructs a nest of sticks, lined with soft materials, and produces from three to five pale bluish-green eggs. Page 129

BALD EAGLE

(*Haliaeetus leucocephalus*)

Length—thirty to thirty-one inches. The sexes are alike in color but the female is larger. The adult female may have a wingspread of as much as seven and one-half feet. The young eagle lacks the conspicuous white head and tail of the adult. This majestic bird nearly disappeared from most of north America as a result of pesticides but is now making a gradual comeback. The diet consists primarily of fish. Eagles mate for life. Their bulky nest is used for many years, the birds adding materials every nesting season until the nest becomes so heavy that it may crash to the ground. Eagles lay two white eggs, occasionally three, at nesting time. Page 133

MOURNING DOVE

(*Zenaida macroura*)

Length—eleven to thirteen inches. The sexes are similar in coloring, except that the female has less iridescence, her breast and forehead being grayish brown. The mourning dove is common over much of North America and is listed as a game bird in some states. In flight the wings make a whistling sound. The call is a soft, repeated *coo*. Mourning doves frequent almost any type of land but apparently prefer cultivated lands, clearings, or spots near houses. They feed mostly on weed seeds and grain. Their nests are flimsy and are built in trees, vines, or shrubs, or very occasionally on the ground. They lay two white eggs at a time and have two or three broods a year. Page 141

BROWN THRASHER

(*Toxostoma rufum*)

Length—ten and one-half to twelve inches. The sexes are alike in color. The brown thrasher's upperparts, wings, and long tail are rufous. It has white wing bars and brown-streaked whitish underparts; the long bill is curved and the eyes are yellow. Thrashers generally inhabit undergrowth, from northern Maine west across southern Canada to Alberta, south to south Florida and the Gulf Coast. Perching on a treetop, the male rivals the mockingbird as he loudly sings his own succession of notes and short phrases interspersed with imitations of other bird calls. The diet is made up mainly of insects, the rest consisting of berries, mast, and grain. The nest is in bushes or thickets and may contain from three to six bluish-white eggs evenly covered with fine brown dots. Usually there are two broods a year. Page 144

GREEN-WINGED TEAL

(*Anas crecca*)

Length—thirteen to fifteen and a half inches. The diminutive size of the green-winged teal is a good fieldmark. The male has an iridescent green speculum on each wing and a green patch on each side of the head that makes it different from the blue-winged teal; both species have brownish spotted and streaked females that look alike with the exception of the green speculum on one and blue shoulder patch on the other. The male utters a short whistle, the female a high-pitched quack. Surface-feeding ducks, green-winged teal haunt ponds and fresh-water marshes, or salt and brackish areas where they can find seeds; other foods are aquatic plants, shellfish, and crustaceans. Green-winged teal winter from southern New England, the Great Lakes, central Montana, and southern Alaska south to the West Indies and Honduras, and breed in southern Canada and northern United States. The nest, usually made near water, is placed in a hollow in grass or in dense vegetation and may contain from six to fourteen cream or greenish-buff eggs. Page 148

KILLDEER

(*Charadrius vociferus*)

Length—nine to eleven inches. Larger than other "ringed" plovers, the killdeer is distinguished by two black breast bands; young birds are paler and have grayish breast bands. The killdeer prefers to be near water but may be seen in pastures, cultivated land, or golf courses. The loud *kill-dee* call is well known; there is also a long, trilling *dee-ee*. Insects and small animal life are this bird's main food. It breeds from southern Canada and New England to the Bahamas, Florida, southern Lower California, and central Mexico, and winters from Illinois and Long Island south to Venezuela and Peru. The nest is a slight depression in the ground, lined with grass, and contains four buff eggs spotted and scrawled with brown. Page 77

NORTHERN ORIOLE

(*Icterus galbula*)

Length—seven to eight inches. In the eastern form of this species, known as the Baltimore oriole, the male is an intense orange and black bird with a white wing bar. The females and young are olive above and yellow below, with two white wing bars; some females have a slight resemblance to males. The whistled song is richly melodic, the call is a single or double whistle, and the young utter a persistent *dee-dee-dee*. Insects, and some fruits, compose the diet. These birds breed from Nova Scotia, Ontario, and southern Manitoba south to northern Georgia, Louisiana, and southern Texas, and west to central Montana and Colorado. They winter in Central America. The nest, a woven bag, is about six inches deep; it is made of light-colored plant fibers and grasses, bark, hair, and string and is suspended from the slender twigs of a branch high in a tall tree. It may contain from four to six white eggs scrawled and blotched at the large end with black and brown. Page 81

PAINTED BUNTING

(*Passerina ciris*)

Length—five and one-quarter inches. The gaudy colors of the adult male are not fully attained for three years; the female is the only plain, greenish, sparrowlike bird in its range; and very young birds are dusky-brown and gray, with whitish underparts. The diet consists mostly of seeds, with some insect matter. A shy and retiring bird, the painted bunting has a cheery warble and sharp call notes. It breeds from North Carolina, Tennessee, Texas, and southern New Mexico south to northern Mexico. It winters from Florida and Mexico to Panama. The nest, in bushes and low trees, is woven of strips of bark, weed stems, grasses, and dead leaves and is lined with soft materials. It may contain three or four white eggs marked with brown. Page 85

RED-WINGED BLACKBIRD

(*Agelaius phoeniceus*)

Length—seven and one-half to nine and one-half inches. The male is black and is easily identifiable because of his red shoulders and yellow shoulder bars. The brownish female is very different in color but is distinguishable because of her broadly striped underparts. The red-wing is very common and may be found in nearly every part of the North American continent. Sometimes these birds can be seen in enormous flocks. The song is *cong-kar-ee-e*, and the alarm note *kack*. The most important food item in the diet is weed seeds, although blackbirds also eat grains and insects. They nest near fresh water, but when the nesting season is over, they are not confined to its vicinity. They make a woven nest on marsh grasses or in bushes, and lay from three to six bluish-white eggs, marked with dark brown or purple. Page 89

BUFFLEHEAD

(*Bucephala albeola*)

Length—thirteen to fifteen inches. One of the smallest ducks, the male bufflehead is mostly white, with a black back and grayish tail; the most conspicuous·mark is the broad white band that passes around the top of the puffy head from eye to eye; the rest of the head, upper neck, and throat are black glossed with purple, greenish and bluish metallic colors. In flight large white wing patches show; when the bird is on water the white sides are particularly conspicuous. The female has a grayish brown head and upperparts. Her underparts are white, and there is a white patch on each side of her head; like the male, she has white wing patches. Diving ducks, buffleheads feed mostly on animal food. They are widely distributed over the continent wherever there are bays, ponds, and sea to afford a suitable habitat for feeding, and in summer, for tree nesting. The male has a rolling guttural note and a soft squeaky call; the female has a hoarse *quack*. The nest is in a stump or tree cavity up to forty feet from the ground and may contain from six to fourteen light buff eggs. Page 101

WOOD DUCK

(*Aix sponsa*)

Length—eighteen to twenty inches. The male wood duck is strikingly marked and highly colored, while the female has a dark crest, white eye-ring and throat. Their most common notes are a high-pitched soft *eeek!* They are found over much of the North American continent. These small river and pond ducks feed on aquatic vegetation but may also wander away from water in search of mast, seeds, and insects. Wood ducks make tree nests in natural cavities, as high as sixty feet from the ground. They lay from ten to fifteen creamy or dull white eggs. Page 105

COMMON RAVEN

(*Corvus corax*)

Length—twenty-two to twenty-six inches. This bulky, blue-black resident of Alaska, Canada, and Greenland goes south to the northern United States and along the Appalachian Mountains to Georgia. It is much larger than the American crow and is unlike the crow in flight, for it alternates flapping with gliding and soaring similar to a vulture. Primarily a scavenger, it is omnivorous. The call is usually a deep croaking, but there is a variety of other gurgling notes. For the nesting site, the pair prefers a cliff but may use a tall tree; the nest is built of sticks and lined with soft materials and may contain from three to seven greenish eggs spotted with brown. Page 109

EASTERN BLUEBIRD

(*Sialia sialis*)

Length—seven inches. This is the only bluebird in the East with a brick-red breast; the female is paler and duller in color. The eastern bluebird can be found in semi-open country and near towns, from south Manitoba, northern Ontario, and Newfoundland to southern Florida and the Gulf Coast, and as far south as Honduras. A beautiful call, *chur-ree*, and several gurgling warbles make up the male's song. The diet is insects and berries. The grass nest is made in tree holes and bird houses and may contain from four to six pale blue eggs. Two broods are raised each year. Page 113